PRAISE FOR *TRAN.*
TEAM WITH THE ENNEAGRAM

What wisdom, what inspiration, and what an exceptional roadmap to create a high-performing team! For years, I have been reflecting and practicing what is and makes a great team. Not ever have I come across an article, let alone a whole book and roadmap, that is such an insightful and comprehensive guide along the way. This is surely a seminal book for all leaders, and I encourage you to start with the top team!

Tex Gunning, CEO, LeasePlan Corporation

There is nothing like the authority of experience, and Ginger Lapid-Bogda has tremendous experience both in guiding people with the Enneagram and with working with teams in major organizations. That experience comes shining through in *Transform Your Team with the Enneagram*, in her clear, compassionate and measured approach to what can be a challenging subject. Ginger takes us through a process of evaluating our team, our own role in that team, and the possible ways the Enneagram may be able to support the team's mission. She takes us through a step-by-step process for using this amazing tool and answers most every question we might have as well as some we might not have considered. I thoroughly enjoyed reading this book and feel it sets new standards for using the Enneagram in organizations. Highly recommended!

Russ Hudson, author of *The Enneagram: Nine Gateways to Presence* and co-author with Don Richard Riso of *The Wisdom of the Enneagram*.

We have struggled for years, like all airlines, with team complexities and challenges emanating from disrupted operations due to technical breakdowns, weather changes and other factors. The Enneagram has gone a long way to help our teams resolve interpersonal problems, improve communication and heighten performance. This book is a must have and read. It is a lifesaver.

Andre Viljoen, Managing Director and CEO, Fiji Airways

Transform Your Team with the Enneagram is an excellent guide and wealth of information for any organization, especially for the individuals that lead teams. Running my own business, I know that understanding my team and our partners is essential to our success. Ginger's ability to break down the process gave me more knowledge and understanding on not only the stages of forming a team but an intimate understanding from the Enneagram's 9 different perspectives. This book illustrates how knowledge of the Enneagram can create more empathy, higher engagement and more understanding in the workplace. Thank you for delivering excellence again!

Meredith Leapley, CEO and founder, Leapley Construction Group

As someone who greatly values the Enneagram, both personally and professionally, I believe this book can certainly help both team members and team leaders improve and accelerate their teams to success and high performance. This book is inspirational, refreshingly approachable in its practicality and very timely. Ginger has created a work of passion that helps you reflect profoundly on your team membership and team leadership behaviors. For me personally, the section on subtypes has helped me to understand and explore this complex set of Enneagram concepts better than ever before.

The insights and exercises are grounded in a true growth mindset. Specifically, the team maps provide a simple yet powerful tool for situational and cultural awareness for both self and team. The development challenges offered for each type create opportunities to stretch oneself in the context of servant leadership and co-creative team membership.

Clint Walker, VP & Global Head of IT Infrastructure Services, Roche/Genentech

Ginger has done it again and given us another valuable resource! As someone who offers team building to a wide range of corporate clients, I appreciate how accessible her book *Transform Your Team with the Enneagram* is and how she brings the concept to life with real life case studies. From CEOs to interns, there is something for everyone in this book.

Pieter Polhuijs, coach, mentor and consultant to start-ups and senior executives

Ginger Lapid-Bogda has brilliantly combined her years of experience as an organizational consultant with her work and writing in the use of the Enneagram to create a book that is a true contribution to the field of team coaching and consulting. This book beautifully combines the stages of team development with the typical behaviors of each Enneagram type at each stage. She provides clear examples of how each Enneagram type responds to each stage and, in so doing, offers ample opportunities for team members to grow individually and as a team. Team coaches and consultants will want this book in their library!

Pam McClean, PhD, Co-Founder & Chief Knowledge Officer, Hudson Institute of Coaching

Ginger is the epitome of practical wisdom of the Enneagram anchored in her depth of experience in working with individuals, teams and organisations. Practical because her knowing and experience are distilled into massively digestible approaches to the challenges found in leading teams and teaming. Wisdom abounds because of the mature heart, hands and head of this remarkably creative and authentic human being. Ginger shares her wealth of knowledge and experience in such a valuable, pragmatic way, it empowers the reader and practitioner with huge insights.

Facilitators, team coaches, team leaders and executives who truly see the importance of knowing self and knowing others will love this book. The dynamics of teams and the teaming journey is supported in this very manageable layout of the book. By recognising the many ego defences that keep teams from making real connections, Ginger guides the reader through the many phases of development and cohesiveness with clarity, focus, attention and grace.

It's a book you will keep by your side in any intervention. To know the Enneagram well is to know yourself well: knowing yourself with clarity and accuracy enables you to navigate the territory of building great teams with greater skill, ease and impact. Thank you Ginger Lapid-Bogda: every time I think I know, despite my wide experience of working with teams over so many years, I learn from you! Inspirational, practical and thought-provoking. It will be by my side!

Dr. Paddy Pampallis, CEO, Integral Africa: The Coaching Centre, Cape Town

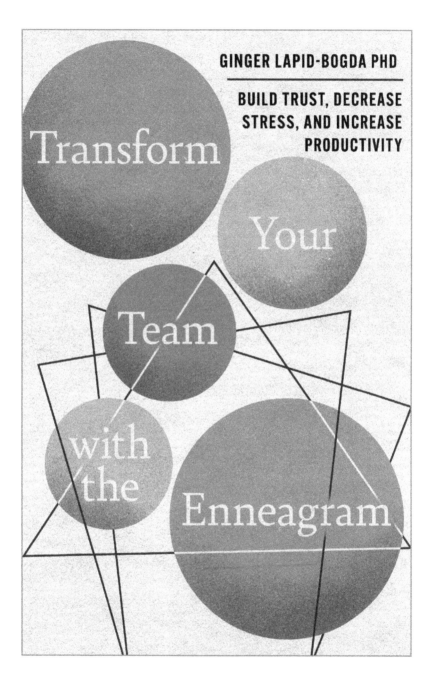

GINGER LAPID-BOGDA PHD

BUILD TRUST, DECREASE
STRESS, AND INCREASE
PRODUCTIVITY

Transform

Your

Team

with
the

Enneagram

The Enneagram in
Business Press

Transform Your Team with the Enneagram
Build Trust, Decrease Stress, and Increase Productivity

Copyright © 2022 by Ginger Lapid-Bogda PhD

Cover design: David Fassett
Interior design: Jeanna Wiggins

ISBN 978-0-9963447-8-4 (print)
ISBN 978-0-9963447-9-1 (digital)

The Enneagram in Business Press
Albany, California

510.570.2971

www.TheEnneagramInBusiness.com

©2022 Ginger Lapid-Bogda PhD

To all the
Enneagram in Business
Network members, who inspire me with their
commitment to the highest quality professional work
with the Enneagram, their pursuit of continuous
personal and professional development,
and their adherence to Blue Ocean
ethical standards

*Each generation will reap
what the former generation has sown.*

—CHINESE PROVERB

● ● ●

TABLE OF CONTENTS

INTRODUCTION

TWO MEMBERS OF A TEAM, both Executive Vice Presidents in a well-known manufacturing organization, could not stand each other.

Their relationship was so bad that they would avoid Executive Committee meetings just so they didn't have to be in the same room at the same time. This caused serious problems for the organization because Jordan was the VP of Quality and Blair was the VP of Manufacturing. Coordination between their two functions was essential to the success of the company. However, they rarely communicated with one another, and, when they did, it was always through curt emails.

Needless to say, their contentious relationship was having an impact — and not in a good way.

Often businesses and organizations are at an impasse; management knows there's an issue between team members but they don't know what to do about it. They know it's not just impacting morale, but it's also impacting the bottom line. The implications of not getting resolution are staggering.

Fortunately, introducing the Enneagram helped resolve this interpersonal problem.

Both Jordan and Blair learned their Enneagram types through coaching. Before coaching with the Enneagram, each believed the other person was the problem. Once they learned the Enneagram, their own types, and how their two types interacted, they realized they were both the issue.

Then one day, Jordan did the previously unimaginable. Knocking on Blair's office door unannounced, Jordan said, "We both know the Enneagram and our types. I think it's time for us to use this understanding to resolve our differences and learn more about each other." They did, and they actually became close friends.

As your emotional intelligence increases, you become more effective, less stressed and easier to work with. The Enneagram is, as Jordan and Blair discovered, the most powerful way to understand yourself and develop your emotional intelligence. The first step is "finding yourself," knowing and accepting who you are. Understanding yourself better, taking responsibility for your own reactions and behaviors, and working on your own personal and professional development help you in all aspects of your life.

On teams, when members truly understand each other, trust builds, stress decreases and teamwork improves. Using the Enneagram is also stimulating and allows people to be more accepting and to navigate difficult conversations in an objective, productive and action-oriented way.

As an organizational consultant for over 45 years, I've consulted to teams in almost every industry and worked with clients such as Salesforce, Apple, Facebook, Kaiser Permanente, and the US Airforce, along with numerous government agencies, law firms, and not-for-profits. I've also worked with many small and medium-size businesses in the retail, service and health care industries. My over four decades of consulting, training or coaching work have almost always involved teams and improving group dynamics at every level.

When you improve interpersonal relationships, you improve productivity and results.

I'd been effectively consulting with hundreds of teams for over 20 years before I learned the Enneagram. Although I had reservations about personality systems in general, I discovered that the Enneagram is far more than a personality system. The Enneagram is ancient wisdom with profound modern applications, including teams. Once I learned the Enneagram, I developed ways to accelerate team development, but also how to use the types on a team to generate team maps.

These maps are the "secret sauce," showing the way for teams to develop in ways they could hardly imagine. This combination of team dynamics and the Enneagram has allowed me to create more productive teams in which team members collaborate and support one another. Even better, it takes half the time at half the cost.

How to create great teams

This book is about how to create great teams using the Enneagram, whatever their size or industry, no matter if the team model is in-person, remote or a hybrid. What you are about to learn will assist you whether you are a team member, a team leader at any organizational level, a coach, trainer or consultant, or if you are simply intrigued by teams.

Someone once asked me if I liked teams since I work with so many of them and know a lot about them. My answer was simple: "I don't like or dislike teams. High-functioning teams have the potential to add enormous value to the organization. Dysfunctional teams harm the work of the organization and cause team members to be ineffective, overly stressed, and to leave the organization. As a result, I want teams to be as effective as possible."

There's almost nothing more exhilarating than being part of a high-performing team and little that is as distressing as being part of a dysfunctional one.

That's why I want to share how to create vibrant, sustainable, high-performing teams.

The guiding insights from the Enneagram show how each of the nine Enneagram types functions at each stage of team development and what people of each type can do to help, rather than hinder, progress to the next stage.

Through a combination of principles from team dynamics, combined with insights from the Enneagram, you'll be amazed, just as I was, how potent using the two together are in creating high-performing teams. Derived from team dynamics, the core principle is that teams go through four predictable stages of team development. If teams address the issues that present themselves at each stage, they can transform from being potential teams to high-performing ones.

Come find out how!

CHAPTER 1

WHY A BOOK ON TEAMS AND THE ENNEAGRAM?

If you want to go fast, go alone.
If you want to go far, go together.

—AFRICAN PROVERB

WHEN I STEPPED INTO THE RECEPTION AREA of the vast, gray concrete building just before meeting my new aerospace client, I was skeptical. They wanted me to do a thorough assessment of a 250-person high-performing team in order to understand what made them so good and what they could do to improve their performance. I wondered, "How can a team so large be so high-performing? Were they really that good?"

When I met the team leader, I was surprised. Jessie was unassuming, quiet and smart. I expected smart, but there was something more important. Jessie's leadership style was an essential ingredient in their high performance.

What I discovered through two months of direct observation and interviews were these keys to the team's success:

A humble, respected leader
The creation of clear work expectations
A deep commitment to team members as people and co-workers
A strong sense of belonging to both the team and the organization

▶	Effective communication strategies
▶	A team culture in which team members felt their voices were respected
▶	Results from their work that were valued by the organization

In addition, I uncovered two more ingredients to this high-performing team. The first was that the team had no "super-stars." In Jessie's own words, "Many team members have the talent to be 'super-stars,' but 'super-stars' come with a price tag; other team members start to function primarily in support of this 'super-star' rather than to support the team as a whole. Also, 'super-stars' come with an attitude of superiority, which is not good for the team." The second ingredient was continuous improvement. The team did not think of itself as a great team, only as a team dedicated to always becoming better. I called both of these ingredients the "no attitude" factor.

In contrast to this team, I also did executive team development work with a three-person executive team from a high-powered, multinational law firm based in New York City. As I gazed upward at their glitzy office building, I wondered what I would encounter. What I found was that this high-level team had more issues than the people in it! Their work in leading their teams was not easy because leading and organizing lawyers is like "herding cats." Like many professions, lawyers are not trained to work on teams, making leading legal teams even more difficult.

There is a Chinese proverb that says, "Fish rots from the head." What is equally true is that executive teams often mirror what lies below them. Teams "above" often duplicate and replicate dysfunction "below."

These executive team members fiercely guarded their individual autonomy, with little value placed on teaming. Even more, their interpersonal dynamic was highly political. Who among them would assume power next? Who had the highest status? Who had the most prestigious clients? Who made the most money?

Theirs was a culture of low trust. I liked and enjoyed each of them individually, but collectively they were dysfunctional. Although my project was ultimately successful, it took much longer and required much deeper work than my work with the much larger, 250-member team.

Trust matters more than size when it comes to team function or dysfunction. And high-functioning teams matter more than ever.

So why is there such an increase in the importance of teams?

Today, teams are everywhere. We work on a variety of teams – think customer service teams, role-based or function-based teams, executive teams, and special project teams, just as starters. Physicians work in teams as do people who work in service delivery. This team trend started over 30 years ago and created a huge team multiplier effect. Now, teams give birth to networks of teams. Here are the key reasons why this is happening.

Globalization: requiring teams to work closer to their clients, geographically and culturally
Function-based teams and sub-teams: providing specific functional products and services
Cross-functional teams: requiring solutions to specific cross-functional issues
Project teams: being created for a specific amount of time to address particular issues
Problem-solving: especially for complex issues needing quick and flexible action
Accelerated workflow speed: requiring increased information sharing and coordination
Global competition: needing even more creativity, innovation and risk-taking

The challenge of today's remote and hybrid team environment

We were already moving to a mixed model of teams, with some teams being remote, some in-person and some a mix of the two, called a hybrid team model. Since the global pandemic caused by COVID 19, even more of us are working in either hybrid teams or entirely remote ones where we might not have ever met our teammates in person. And it appears that this trend will continue whether or not the pandemic continues.

Here's why. We've learned how to work remotely, the technology now available supports remote work, organizations have either hired people who live in remote locations or current employees have moved away because they could work remotely, and remote workers often save organizations money: less office space, less furniture.

With all the benefits, remote work also comes at a price. Teamwork becomes even more important, but high-functioning teams do not just happen magically even when these teams are in-person teams. And high-performing remote or hybrid teams are even more complicated to create and sustain.

Here's why. We no longer see and engage with teammates in real time. Going to lunch with one another or having informal conversations with each other – these used to be called "water cooler" conversations, but now could be "coffee bar" conversations – just don't happen with hybrid and remote teams. This raises more questions:

How do we learn to "read" other team members' reactions or concerns when we are primarily communicating in front of computer screens viewing one another from the shoulders upward?
How do we ensure enough psychological safety so that team members feel comfortable engaging authentically with one another, especially when their proximity to each other is so limited?
How do team leaders provide the right amount of clarity, structure, communication and accountability without over- or under-managing teams?
How do teams navigate important team issues such as inclusion and trust, always a team issue, but even more important in hybrid and remote teams?

Whether your team works remotely, meets in-person, or functions as a hybrid, the fundamentals of creating a transformed team are essentially the same. Teamwork always mattered, but now it matters even more!

Return to old watering holes for more than water;
friends and dreams are there to meet you.

—AFRICAN PROVERB

CHAPTER 2

WHAT IS A TEAM AND HOW IS IT DIFFERENT FROM A GROUP?

A house is not a home.

—ENGLISH PROVERB

MANY PEOPLE USE THE WORDS GROUP AND TEAM interchangeably. But a group is not necessarily a team, just like a house is not always a home! A team is a very specific type of group, and not all groups are or even should be teams.

What is a group?

Tracy, Vice President of Support Services for a global non-profit, had seven direct reports. What did these group members have in common other than reporting to the VP of Support Services? The answer is nothing, except that they all provided different kinds of services to other organizational units – logistics, finance, innovation, among others.

Tracy tried to make them a team, spending thousands of dollars on team building activities and leading three-hour meetings every month so that each member could share what they were working on. As hard as Tracy tried, nothing formed them into a team. There was a simple reason for this. They were simply a group of individuals who needed to report to someone in the organization.

They were not a team and never could be. Here's why.

A "group" is a collection of individuals that have something in common. For example, group members might share a common interest – a club, a cause, a committee – or they may report to the same person in the organization, just because the organization needs them to report somewhere. However, group members don't need to work together to achieve their goals.

Group members may even do activities together, but this does not make them a team. Spending time getting to know one another, to celebrate events such as holidays and birthdays, or to be part of a training program still has value. These activities can be enjoyable, increase peoples' skills, and create goodwill within the organization. However, shared experiences do not make a group a team.

What is a possible team?

The first kind of team is a "possible team." This "possible team" has the unrealized potential of becoming an "actual team" if they can (1) identify one or more common team goals and (2) have some degree of interdependence for accomplishing these goals. Without a common goal or goals and some degree of interdependence for achieving these goals, at least among some team members, this collection of individuals is a group and will always struggle to be a team.

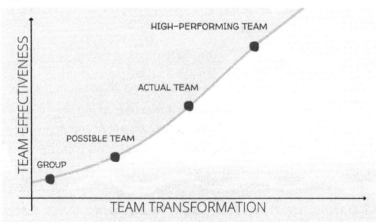

What about interdependence?

Teams that have too little interdependence, compared to what they really need, will be ineffective.

Think of a soccer team, a team that requires high interdependence among its players to win the game. A soccer team that operates as if each player is independent from the others will rarely move a ball across the field or score many goals.

Teams with too much interdependence, more than is actually required, become inefficient.

Think of a golf team, a team in which each team member operates independently during play, with the one common goal being the collective low scores needed to win the tournament. The golf team may have a positive team spirit, which is a good thing, but too much interdependence will not help them win the tournament. In fact, it will take up time that is better spent on individual practice.

For example, I worked for several years as a consultant to a major international accounting firm that also provided business consulting to their accounting clients. My role was to facilitate new teams of 36 business consultants from across the globe.

Their assigned task was to work with a real client on a real consulting project. They had to complete their consulting project within two weeks, with a deliverable determined through negotiations with their client. The deliverable was always big and ambiguous, and we gave these "possible teams" few guidelines about how to organize themselves. This was an intentional part of their learning; we wanted them to learn how to form high-performing teams themselves.

Many teams met this challenge with great success; a few did not.

The successful teams always spent time identifying their common goals and establishing effective interdependencies before they organized themselves to do the actual work.

The unsuccessful teams rushed right into their project work and immediately organized themselves into sub-teams. These teams always thought they were great teams because they were action-oriented. But they never became truly high-performing because they typically collapsed into disarray halfway through the project. The teams argued without resolving their conflicts; the sub-teams of the larger team did not have clear directions and did not coordinate their work with each other; and team members were constantly challenging each other's leadership. In short, these "possible teams" never became "actual teams."

What is an actual team?

An "actual team" is more evolved than a "possible team." It is more advanced because it has clearly identified and agreed upon common goals and the optimal level of interdependence required for their team to be effective and efficient. In addition, teams that have progressed from "possible teams" to "actual teams" have the following qualities, at least to some degree:

Technical or functional expertise
A range of skills within the team that addresses all of the work needing to be done.

Problem-solving and decision-making skills
An ability to identify and solve issues and challenges as they arise, as well as to make effective and timely decisions.

Interpersonal skills
Team members listen to each other, plus communicate and address conflict effectively. They also give useful feedback and offer other team members support and recognition.

Here's an example of a "potential team" struggling to be an "actual team." This 10-person team provided learning and development activities for the Information Technology (IT) division of a Fortune 500 company. The team's purpose, goals and optimal interdependencies were clear and understood by all team members. Overall, clients valued their services. However, the team had challenges working together.

Although their technical skills were excellent, their problem-solving and decision-making skills were not. The reason for this was that Leigh, their team leader, micromanaged all aspects of problem-solving and decision-making.

Micromanaging almost always disempowers team members and keeps a "potential team" from developing into an "actual team." It stops team members from being fully empowered to all go in the same direction.

What is a high-performing team?

A "high-performing team" shares all the characteristics of an "actual team," yet there is more. A "high-performing" team also has these qualities:

Customer-focused

Their primary focus is on providing value to the customer and secondarily on the satisfaction of team members.

A boat doesn't go forward if each one is rowing their own way.

—SWAHILI PROVERB

Increasingly high levels of expertise and skills

Team members' areas of expertise and skills operate at increasingly higher levels of effectiveness: technical or functional expertise, problem-solving and decision-making skills, and interpersonal skills.

Resilient

They are resilient, able to respond to changes and challenges in agile and innovative ways.

Culture of support and development

Team members actively support the growth and development of each other, encouraging one another's success and recognition.

Reilly's team would never describe itself as a "high-performing team," although everyone else in their organization did. Each of the 15 team members knew what they were doing and why. They placed the customer first, actively supported each other in their work, collaborated as needed, and were deeply committed to increasing their learning as individuals and as a team.

When Reilly asked me to facilitate a team assessment to determine how they could improve their performance, they scored high on every dimension assessed. Reilly was stunned and emotional seeing the results. What Reilly saw was a team that deeply cared about their work and each other. Even more, they viewed Reilly as just the right leader for what they needed.

What I saw in action were the three principles I'd learned from the 250-person team described in chapter one: a humble leader, a "no-attitude" team culture, and a commitment to continuous learning.

Where do you start?

Determine if yours is a group or a team; if a team, first clarify common goals and optimal level of interdependence. You have to start at the beginning.

If you want to know the end, look at the beginning.

—AFRICAN PROVERB

GREAT IDEAS

A GROUP OR A TEAM?

GREAT IDEA | What to do with a group that is not yet a team

Start by having the group identify at least one goal all members have in common by asking them. If they can't find one, then don't try to do team building or team development activities with them. There are many activities they might do together that they can enjoy and would perceive as rewards.

GREAT IDEA | How to identify common goals

 "Possible teams" need to first identify their team's purpose, sometimes referred to as the "team charter." What are they being asked to accomplish? Why were they created? What does the organization expect of them? Once team members understand their team purpose, the next step is to identify the most important team goals, usually more than one and not more than five.

GREAT IDEA | How to determine optimal level of team interdependence

How much interdependence does your team need to be most effective and efficient? First, identify the interdependencies for each goal. Second, for each goal, assess whether the interdependencies are too many, too few or not the right ones. Finally, make changes as needed.

Go to Resources for more ideas and details.

THE ENNEAGRAM

I found myself.

—RUMI (13ᵀᴴ CENTURY PERSIAN POET)

HAVE YOU EVER WONDERED why people say one of these things?

You appear critical in your word choice, voice tone, and body language
You smile most of the time and offer frequent advice
You get impatient easily and let people know when their time is up
You seem overly sensitive and need to take things less personally
You are remote and distant so they can't "read" your reactions
You ask too many questions that get in the way of forward momentum
You need to be more focused and stay "on point"
You intimidate them even when you are not trying to do this
You are so easy-going, but they don't know what you really think

Find out why through the Enneagram!

The Enneagram, an ancient system at least 2000-4000 years old, accurately describes nine different human character structures, shown on the symbol as numbers one through nine. Each type has distinct patterns of thinking, feeling and behaving, as well as a unique worldview and motivational structure. And because the Enneagram is both deep and dynamic, it is as profound as it is powerful.

THE NINE ENNEAGRAM TYPES ON TEAMS

So how do the nine types function on teams? The Enneagram can predict this well because each type has strong preferences about what they want from a team and from other team members.

Before describing each Enneagram type, I want to share my own reaction to "personality systems."

I have over four decades of experience as an organization development consultant and am a trained Gestalt therapist. Because of this, I understand and have used almost all of the "personality systems" currently available. In my view, some are more accurate and useful than others.

What I don't like about most "personality systems" is that they tend to reduce people to categories. People are more complex than categories or labels. The Enneagram doesn't fall into the trap of making people into less than they are.

As one of my clients said so well, "The Enneagram doesn't put you into a box. It shows you the box you are in and how to move beyond this."

Here are the nine Enneagram types described in the context of what they like from team members and how they function in team settings.

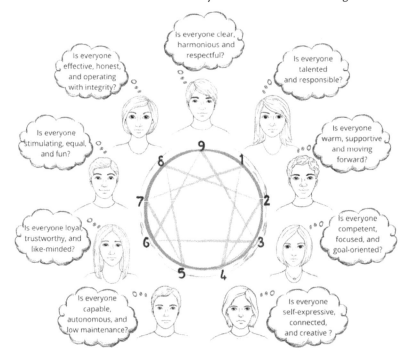

Enneagram One

Why do Enneagram Ones place such a high value on teams that have talented and responsible team members? They believe that when people are talented and responsible, the team's work will be of the highest quality and also get done on time. This is important to them because Ones want everything and everyone, including themselves, to be as perfect as possible and everything to be done with no mistakes. To that end, Ones hold themselves and others to the highest standards of excellence.

They take strong positions based on their opinions and judgments and believe that their approach is the right way in terms of how a team should be organized to move forward. They also believe their solutions are the best ones and tend to be more highly structured, detailed-oriented and self-controlled than other people.

More task than relationship-oriented, Ones believe in following the rules. However, not all Ones have the exact same rules. That said, Ones do believe these two things: (1) everyone should be continuously engaged in self-improvement, and (2) we should always be polite because it's especially impolite to show anger.

COULD YOU BE AN ENNEAGRAM ONE?
▶ Do you believe that if it's not worth doing right, it's not worth doing?
▶ Do you think that there is almost always one right way to do things?
▶ Do you think it's not OK to express anger, so you call it frustration, upset or irritation instead?
▶ Do you have trouble delegating because you think no one can do it as correctly or as well as you?

Enneagram Two

Why do Enneagram Twos place such a high value on teams that are warm, supportive and moving forward? That's because Twos work best on teams that have these characteristics and think others do, too. They

also believe that people achieve their highest performance when they feel included, particularly when everyone is valued and going in the same direction.

Twos often act like team cheerleaders, motivating others to feel good and believe in themselves. They do this by paying close attention to what people want, need and feel, an ability Twos say is intuitive and comes naturally to them. Twos don't understand why others don't pay enough attention to body language and what people really mean by what they say.

More relationship-oriented than task-focused, Twos are warm, friendly, and good listeners, liking to give advice as a way of helping others. It is also extremely important to them that they are perceived as kind, generous, thoughtful and selfless rather than selfish.

COULD YOU BE AN ENNEAGRAM TWO?
Are relationships extremely important to you and always have been?
Are you really good at asking people questions as a way to get to know them better?
Do you continuously read other people's verbal and nonverbal communications and do this intuitively and accurately?
Are you an optimistic person, particularly when thinking about other people and their potential?

Enneagram Three

Why do Enneagram Threes place such a high value on all team members being competent, focused and goal-oriented? It's because Threes are driven by the need to succeed and equally driven by the need to avoid failure. They believe that teams with competent, focused and goal-oriented members set the stage for everyone's success.

Is everyone competent, focused, and goal-oriented?

Threes set specific goals for everything they want to achieve, create efficient and effective plans for getting there, and then move forward quickly. To them, moving forward is its own reward, but standing still is the same as being idle.

They also like a healthy competition because they like winning and sharpening their skills. At the same time, they'd rather lose to a superior team than beat a clearly inferior one. There's no joy in beating an ineffective team but have a lot to learn from testing themselves against a better one.

Threes are also good at reading their audience and adjusting how they present themselves in order to get a positive response. They know how to change their clothing, adapt their speaking style, and shift their body language in order to get the reaction they desire.

COULD YOU BE AN ENNEAGRAM THREE?
Do you create goals and plans easily and feel lost if you don't have these?
Are you good at reading your audience and making adjustments as needed?
Do you believe your value comes from what you do and accomplish?
Do you focus on work and tasks and think that dealing with emotions for too long is a waste of time?

Enneagram Four

Why do Enneagram Fours place such a high value on team environments where everyone is self-expressive, connected and creative? This is the exact team culture in which Fours thrive.

Fours go deeply into just about everything they do. This can be work, relationships, special interests they may have, or aesthetic areas such as art and literature. They believe that almost everything has meaning if you just go below the surface and explore things in depth.

Fours are also highly sensitive to interactions with others. This leads them to be finely tuned to other people as well as to themselves. They need to find passion in their work and support others to do this, too.

In addition, their original thinking and creativity help them "think outside the box" in terms of approaching issues and problem-solving. This can also cause them to feel very different from others and not fully part of a team.

Fours get easily bored by repetitive tasks and superficial conversations. They want to keep everything real and deep.

COULD YOU BE AN ENNEAGRAM FOUR?

▷ Do you think of yourself as original, one of a kind, so that no one is quite like you?

▷ Are you introspective and like spending time exploring your inner world of thoughts and feelings?

▷ Do you believe you are what you feel, even though your feelings change regularly?

▷ Are you good at and enjoy helping others explore their feelings and experiences in great depth?

Enneagram Five

Why do Enneagram Fives place such a high value on teams where everyone is capable, autonomous and low maintenance? It's simply because they view themselves as competent and capable, competence defined as being knowledgeable and also understanding how things work. Fives also value these qualities in their teammates.

Is everyone capable, autonomous, and low maintenance?

Autonomy is a professional and personal issue for Fives. Although they contribute to teams as needed, they do not like what they consider to be excessive meetings or over-coordination. They find both to be energy-depleting and a waste of time.

In addition, Fives do not like being micro-managed or under a microscope when they work with others. They prefer that people leave them alone so they can do their work. Their focus is on research, planning and executing what is doable, manageable and practical.

They work best with people who are low maintenance, which means non-demanding, non-intrusive, and not highly emotional. Requests for too much of their time feel like a demand, personal questions feel intrusive, and emotionally charged discussions feel unproductive and draining.

COULD YOU BE AN ENNEAGRAM FIVE?

▷ Do you guard your privacy closely, sharing information about yourself with only a few select people?

▶	Is it important to you that people respect your personal space and do not sit or stand too close to you?
▶	Do you not experience most feelings in real time, but process and reflect on them later when you are alone?
▶	Do you believe logic is objective and trustworthy, but view emotions as too subjective?

Enneagram Six

Why do Enneagram Sixes place such a high value on teams where everyone is loyal, trustworthy and like-minded? Teams with these characteristics help Sixes feel comfortable and safe. Safety is central to Sixes because they view the world as an uncertain, unpredictable place. There is, in their view, safety in numbers rather than in being an isolated individual.

Like-minded doesn't mean "group-think" or conformism. It's more about shared values and a commitment to the team. In fact, Sixes are prone to ask questions that challenge the way the team functions or decisions are made. They also like it when others do the same. Their questions often start with "What if" and are intended to help the team consider possible outcomes before moving forward.

Think of Sixes as realistic idealists. They hope for the best and are also aware that obstacles appear that get in the way of advancement. If these obstacles can be identified in advance and planned for, they believe things will then move in a positive direction. Sixes think of themselves as creative problem-solvers who enjoy complex challenges.

COULD YOU BE AN ENNEAGRAM SIX?	
▶	Do you like to think through various contingencies before you take action?
▶	Do you calculate risk on an ongoing basis, being risk-avoidant, risk-approaching or both?
▶	Do you have a very active mind that is hard to keep still and calm?
▶	Are you a loyal and responsible person, particularly with those close to you or teams to which you belong?

Enneagram Seven

Why do Enneagram Sevens place such a high value on team environments where everyone is stimulating, equal and fun? Sevens thrive in highly engaging, exciting and pleasurable work settings. They despair in environments that are routine, boring and restrictive. Sevens believe in infinite possibilities, thinking anything is possible with both the right people and the fewest limitations.

Is everyone stimulating, equal, and fun?

Sevens rarely ask "Why?" Instead, they say, 'Why not!" They are energetic and enthusiastic and believe it is their job to keep themselves and everyone else upbeat and optimistic.

In team settings, they often tell jokes or say something amusing when they think the conversation is getting too serious. If something is not going as desired or someone is displeased with them, they reframe the situation and make it seem highly positive. For example, if the team lost a desirable client, a Seven might say, "They wouldn't have stayed as a client for very long, and we now have the resources to get three new clients instead of one."

They also love generating new ideas and creating innovative solutions to existing problems.

COULD YOU BE AN ENNEAGRAM SEVEN?
Do you think being positive is always a choice and so you choose to be positive at almost all times?
Do you get feedback from others that they feel interrupted by you when you are actually saying something because you are excited by an idea?
Do you believe nobody has the right to restrict or limit you?
Is it hard for you to stay with your emotions for long periods of time, especially sadness and fear?

Enneagram Eight

Is everyone effective, honest, and operating with integrity?

Why do Enneagram Eights place such a high value on teams where everyone is effective, honest and operating with integrity? When their teammates have these qualities, Eights do not have to be concerned about the performance or character of anyone on their team. When Eights can count on their team-mates to do their jobs well, Eights believe the team can move to action with everyone going in the same direction.

For Eights, integrity has many components: doing what you say you will do, no manipulation, taking responsibility for your behavior rather than blaming someone else, and telling the truth. Eights simply do not like un-necessary surprises or deception.

They tend to be bold, confident, and strategic and like to be a part of big action that has a large impact. They don't like to be bothered with details or actions that are relatively unimportant.

Even when they are not the team leader, Eights will step in to assert control if they believe that the team is not going in the right direction. They also tend to have big energy and a strong exterior that covers up their vulnerability.

COULD YOU BE AN ENNEAGRAM EIGHT?
Do you think that bigger is better, both in thought and action, as long as it is also strategic?
Are you a direct and assertive person who can intimidate people even when this may not be your intention?
Do you trust your "gut" responses in almost everything you decide or do?
Do you have a bold exterior and have a difficult time both experiencing and showing others when you feel vulnerable?

Enneagram Nine

Why do Enneagram Nines place such a high value on teams where everyone is clear about what they are supposed to do, there's maximum harmony and minimum tension, and people are respectful of one another? Nines believe that when everyone is clear about what is expected, tensions will be minimal; Nines are extremely tension sensitive and experience disharmonious relationships in their bodies. Theirs is a strong somatic response to unresolved issues, brewing conflict or any source of team tension.

Is everyone clear, harmonious and respectful?

They also view respect as an essential ingredient for positive, harmonious team interactions. For Nines, lack of respect is the same as rudeness. In the Nine's view, not asking for or listening to everyone's opinion is rude and disrespectful. Asserting yourself is not only rude, it's also pushy and aggressive.

In addition, Nines are highly conflict-avoidant when they are directly involved. At the same time, they are excellent mediators when the conflict involves others because they are good listeners, non-judgmental, are open to different points of view, and are skilled at helping others find "common ground."

COULD YOU BE AN ENNEAGRAM NINE?
Do you wish everyone could live in a world of mutual respect, minimal tension and limited conflict?
Do you have trouble knowing and expressing what you do want, but are better at knowing what you don't want?
Do people tell you that you are highly approachable and very easy to talk to?
Do you dislike pressure to have to do something and find yourself saying "yes" rather than "no" as a way to keep the peace?

What is the best way to discover your Enneagram type?

There are many ways to discover your Enneagram type. The most important thing to keep in mind is that you need to be actively involved in the discovery. You can't rely on an outside expert – a book, a test or a teacher – to tell you who you are. You need to uncover your type yourself.

Of course, you want the best method and highest quality guidance possible. The methods you can choose from include Enneagram tests, presentations and lectures, typing cards, typing interviews, books, apps and websites, and type panels.

Here's a short description of each approach. Each method has its pros and cons, and often several approaches are used together.

Enneagram tests

I don't use Enneagram tests, primarily because they are, at best, 65-70% accurate. Why? The Enneagram types are multi-dimensional and are not only about behaviors or traits, which is what tests primarily measure.

In addition, several Enneagram types behave similarly and also share certain qualities. Your type is actually about your patterns of thinking, feeling and behaving, as well as what motivates or drives your patterns.

Some trainers do use tests, but they usually let you know that the test is just the beginning of the conversation about your type and not a definitive answer. They then help you clarify whether or not the test result was accurate.

Presentations and lectures
Presentations and lectures are an important way to learn Enneagram content, and this can be through webinars, podcasts, videos, eLearning platforms and in-person lectures. Just make sure that whoever you are learning from knows the Enneagram accurately and conveys the types without stereotyping or judging any of the types as good, bad or better than the other types. Find someone you think you can learn from.

Typing cards
I teach the Enneagram and the nine types through both presentation and typing cards. Once people understand the Enneagram system and types, they then place nine different cards into three piles; *yes*, most likely their type; *no*, not their type; or *maybe*, meaning possibly their type. Finally, they rank order their *yes* pile. Each full-color card describes an Enneagram type with a paragraph description and illustration. Our typing cards are available to the public; there are also other providers available.

Typing interviews
Individual typing interviews take about one hour, during which time you answer a series of questions. It takes a highly experienced and well-trained typing interviewer to do this well; quality and experience matter.

This method works well for coaching and also in executive teams if executive team members prefer this. For larger groups or teams, individual typing interviews can be expensive, plus other group or team members miss out on learning about each person's type in a more transparent setting.

Books, apps and websites
Some people identify their type through reading Enneagram books, going to websites containing Enneagram information or via smartphone apps. If

this learning method works well for you, just make sure you go to multiple reliable sources. With so many Enneagram books currently available, some are much better than others.

Type panels

Enneagram type panels are small groups of people of the same type who are interviewed by a trained Enneagram facilitator. To find your type, you observe a type panel and then assess if you are similar to people on the panel.

It's a good way to hear themes from people of the same type, observe their similarities in body language, and pick up other type-based themes and clues.

Should you have all 9 Enneagram types on your team?

When I teach the Enneagram to groups and to teams, I regularly get asked these two questions:

1. Should we hire people by type if we are missing these types on our team or in our organization?

2. What are the best type pairings for romantic relationships?

The answer to both questions is the same. *Do not make these kinds of decisions based on Enneagram type.*

Hiring decisions should be made based on skills and experience relevant to the job because Enneagram type has no correlation to skills, experience or job success.

The same is true for romance. Romantic pairings based on type only predict why the two individuals might be drawn to one another in the first place and, even more predictively, what they will disagree about and fight about in the future. Select romantic partners based on their self-mastery level, the higher the better for both you and them. You'll fight less, enjoy each other more and not blame each other when things don't go well.

Similarly, hire team members based on skills, relevant experience and self-mastery level, not based on type.

Why self-mastery matters for hiring and not type

What is the greatest predictor of success in every occupation and industry across the globe? The answer is emotional intelligence!

Research has proved this to be true for over three decades. Of course, relevant skills and experience also matter. You can think of emotional intelligence as self-mastery.

What is self-mastery? It's a combination of eight factors, from self-awareness to a commitment to lifelong learning.

Self-awareness	Awareness of patterns of thoughts, feelings and behaviors as well as your true motivations and your impact on others
Receptivity to feedback	Able to effectively use positive and negative feedback from others even if it is not given in the way you prefer or given from those whose feedback you don't value
Taking responsibility for your own reactions	Take responsibility for yourself without blaming others and being able to accurately assess what is your responsibility and what is that of other people
Motivation	Intrinsically motivated rather than motivated by fear or by external rewards
Self-management	Able to make conscious choices about your responses rather than controlling them or over-expressing them
Emotional maturity	Make wise and thoughtful choices, displaying inner wisdom and guidance
Personal vision	Have a compelling sense of purpose with underlying positive values
Commitment to lifelong learning	Engage in self-development on an ongoing basis and not just under stress

Self-mastery means knowing yourself, taking responsibility for reactions, relating to others in productive ways, and being committed to your ongoing personal and professional development.

As you look at the self-mastery graph, you can see there are different levels of self-mastery: low, moderate and high.

The best team members are at the moderate self-mastery level or above. People in the lower self-mastery ranges are reactive, tend to blame others rather than acknowledge their own role in different situations, and create more stress for other team members.

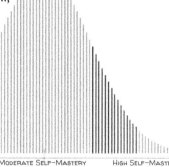

LOW SELF-MASTERY   MODERATE SELF-MASTERY   HIGH SELF-MASTERY

Jean, a human resource director in charge of recruitment, said this to a group of managers, "Honestly, how many of you have made a wrong hire decision based on the person's technical skills and experience? Not me and not you! Wrong hires are almost always because the person could not get along with people, they only cared about themselves, or they lied about everything." Everyone smiled in recognition; nobody disagreed.

The cost of a wrong hire is expensive; in key positions, a wrong hire costs the equivalent of one year's salary; in senior executive positions, the cost can be the equivalent of two year's salary; in more junior positions, the cost can be 30% of an annual salary or more. This is just the pure financial loss. The cost to productivity and morale can be even higher.

The Enneagram is the most powerful way to increase self-mastery. It is also intriguing, illuminating and fun.

In addition, once people know their Enneagram types, the system provides specific development activities for people of each type, targeting exactly what they most desire to change, whether personal or professional. It's also a potent way to work with teams, going way beyond the personal and professional development of team members.

The Enneagram illuminates how teams actually work.

Better a diamond with a flaw than a pebble without one.

—CHINESE PROVERB

CHAPTER 4

HOW TO USE THE ENNEAGRAM FOR GROUP COHESION AND TEAM BUILDING

If you don't know where you are going,
then any road will do.

—TIBETAN PROVERB

AS I BEGAN THE FIRST OF four virtual sessions with "Prestigious Consulting, Inc." (not their real name), I felt excited and concerned. Forty experienced professionals who wanted to understand the Enneagram more deeply and how to use it more effectively with their clients.

My excitement came with a caution. They called themselves "prestigious," but by what standard: money charged, high status of their clients? I didn't know.

They also called themselves a "team," when they were actually a group, not a team. They rarely worked together on projects and had no common goals.

But whether they were a team or a group didn't matter for the program itself. They wanted an Enneagram training with applications to coaching and training, and I could deliver that. Or so I thought!

The first session went well; they were responsive and curious. The second session went even better, even though they did not want to follow the agreed-upon agenda. They wanted to discuss how culture impacts type and how type impacts how people of each type think, feel, and behave in different cultures.

The problem for me was I no longer knew what to do in sessions three and four. The plan was to do session three on coaching with the Enneagram and the final session on Enneagram training activities. Because they had changed the agenda for session two, I asked them what they wanted for the final two sessions. Their response was ambiguous; some people wanted one topic and others wanted to cover other items.

There was no consensus, so I tried my best, but the overall program result was just OK. Why? Because they really didn't know why they wanted to learn the Enneagram.

This is always the most important question to answer: why does a team or group want to learn about and use the Enneagram? If there is a clear answer to this question, then there are two more that need to be answered.

> Is there enough psychological safety to introduce the Enneagram?
>
> Are there issues that need to be addressed before introducing the Enneagram?

What is your purpose for using the Enneagram?

Here are some great reasons to use the Enneagram for you to look over. This can help you identify what your purpose might be, in addition to increasing skills in sales, strategy, influence, motivation, creativity, innovation, risk-taking, decision making, as examples.

GREAT REASONS TO USE THE ENNEAGRAM		
Helping people grow personally	Developing leaders	Motivating people
Helping people develop professionally	Communicating more effectively	Changing company culture
Creating greater cohesion and inclusion	Managing conflict constructively	Retaining employees
Enhancing teamwork	Instilling a feedback culture	Introducing something new and stimulating

Is there enough psychological safety within the group or team to use the Enneagram?

You might want to use the Enneagram, but is it the right time?

Psychological safety is a key factor and is even more important in remote or hybrid groups and teams because of the social distance and the increased challenge of getting to know and trust one another. Psychological safety is the belief that you won't be humiliated or punished for sharing your thoughts and feelings. It also means that people feel safe to take personal and interpersonal risks with each other. When people feel safe, they are willing to be more vulnerable and share more.

A group or team doesn't have to have a 100% psychologically safe environment for the Enneagram to work well. It does require enough psychological safety for people to be willing to explore themselves in a setting with other people. They also need to believe that what they share and whatever their Enneagram type is will not be used against them in any way.

Psychological safety and trust are intertwined. The more psychological safety, the more trust. The less psychological safety, the less trust.

Use the Psychological Safety Assessment to rate your team.

PSYCHOLOGICAL SAFETY ASSESSMENT	LOW	MEDIUM			HIGH
Do people feel free to share their thoughts and feelings?	1	2	3	4	5
Is the overall trust level high?	1	2	3	4	5
Is the atmosphere non-judgmental and supportive?	1	2	3	4	5
Do people feel valued and respected?	1	2	3	4	5
Do people disagree with each other in productive ways?	1	2	3	4	5
Is risk-taking encouraged even if you make a mistake?	1	2	3	4	5
Is there an absence of scapegoating and blame?	1	2	3	4	5

WHAT YOUR SCORES MEAN

Moderate to high scores

3-5 range scores: moderate to high levels of psychological safety and trust; ideal for introducing the Enneagram

1-2 range scores: low levels of psychological safety and trust; address the sources of these low scores before you introduce the Enneagram

Mixed to low scores

Mixed high and low scores: address a few specific issues before you introduce the Enneagram

Please remember that people may look and act like everything is fine when it is not. People may not feel safe enough to even say what they are truly thinking and feeling. While the Enneagram can be used in almost any organizational application, serious underlying issues need to be addressed before the Enneagram can be used effectively with a group or team.

The teeth are smiling, but is the heart?

—CONGO PROVERB

Are there issues that need to be addressed before you introduce the Enneagram to a group or team?

Both lack of psychological safety and low trust are symptoms of something deeper. Causes of low psychological safety and deep distrust can be about leadership style, scapegoating, preferential treatment, or inclusion-exclusion issues, just as examples.

These difficult issues usually need to be addressed before introducing the Enneagram. The Enneagram is extraordinarily useful in helping people know and understand themselves and others better and to increase skills in communication, leadership and managing conflict. But if you bring it to a group or team where there is deep-rooted tension and conflict, the Enneagram alone cannot solve it and might even make the situation worse.

If there are significant issues that need to be addressed before introducing the Enneagram, groups and teams need a professional trainer who knows the Enneagram well and also has excellent consulting skills. Trainers are trained to design and lead structured learning. Consultants are trained to help clients diagnose and solve real issues in real time.

I received a request for Enneagram work with a not-for-profit team that explains this issue clearly.

Taylor, the Executive Director of an organization involved in combatting human trafficking, called to ask me to lead an Enneagram program for the staff. When I asked about the purpose of this work, Taylor shared a steady stream of issues facing the organization: the recent firing of several key staff members; intense, ongoing conflict between two other staff members; challenges to Taylor's leadership, such as certain staff not following through on requests and making aggressive comments during team meetings; and longer-term team members ganging up on newer staff members.

On top of these issues, the organization had just received a big funding grant and needed to expand its current services by 300% within the next year. Oh, my!

I explained to Taylor that her initial request could backfire on her and the organization. In other words, there wasn't enough psychological safety and trust to use the Enneagram with the staff. It was likely that they would not be willing to explore themselves and share their types with one another.

Even worse, it was possible that some or all of their issues would emerge in the team setting without any ground rules or structure to support a positive outcome. The underlying issues needed to get identified and resolved prior to bringing in the Enneagram.

Here's the steps we took with Taylor's team based on the identification of the team's underlying issues. All of the steps involved the Enneagram:

STEP ONE	Weekly coaching for Taylor for 6 months

Taylor was in a high-stress leadership role, and an executive coach offered support and clarity, in a confidential setting, to examine Taylor's leadership style and what Taylor needed to change: re-establish Taylor's leadership authority, instill confidence among the staff because they could see changes in Taylor's leadership style, and help Taylor regain self-confidence.

As an Enneagram Six, Taylor's leadership and decision-making were inconsistent. Sometimes the right decisions were made too late; at times, wrong decisions were made too early.

STEP TWO	Conflict resolution between two staff members

Using a consultant adept at resolving conflict, the Enneagram was used to help the two staff members in conflict understand themselves and the other person better, to take responsibility for their own reactivity and the negative impact on their interpersonal dynamics, and to also identify and resolve other organization issues that were causing the conflict between them.

STEP THREE	Planning for upcoming expansion

The 300% expansion needed a practical plan. As a type Six, Taylor tended to over-plan as a way to cover all possible ways something could go wrong. Using the Enneagram and with the help of the coach, Taylor was able to simplify the plan, which reduced everyone's stress level.

STEP FOUR	Enneagram program for entire staff

Once the main organizational issues above were visibly improving, there was more than enough psychological safety and trust for the staff to learn the Enneagram and apply their insights to their own development and teamwork.

Should you use an experienced Enneagram trainer or consultant to work with your team?

If you want to build high, you must dig deep.

—MONGOLIAN PROVERB

The answer: most probably, *yes.*

First, Enneagram-trained professionals know the Enneagram system and how to help people identify their types. Without accurate type identification, you can't apply the Enneagram to any area such as leadership, teamwork or communication.

Second, an experienced trainer or consultant should have the skills to help you determine your program goals, design the program or consultation project, and be able to assist you in implementation.

Here are some areas that need your attention in choosing an experienced Enneagram professional.

| Case One | An Enneagram teacher may know the Enneagram but not be skilled at using it in an organizational setting |

Chris is an Enneagram teacher who is also an accomplished author. What Chris doesn't have is experience in organizations either as an employee or as a trainer or consultant. So when a Fortune 50 company contacted Chris to teach a high-level team the Enneagram and communication skills, Chris said *yes* but should have said *no*.

The program didn't go well because Chris made three "rookie" mistakes.

The first mistake involved using an Enneagram test prior to the session as the primary way for participants to find their types.

The second mistake was Chris following the test with four hours of lecture on the types. Chris made the assumption that people who were incorrectly typed by the test would self-correct just by hearing a lecture. They didn't.

The third mistake was to teach each of the types using off-putting language. Chris described each type as being deeply wounded or traumatized with a specific "core wound."

I heard this story because the same client asked me to work with this team to do a typing "do-over." The client also said, "Please don't use 'core wound' in our company. That is way too psychological, and can I ask you, are we all so deeply traumatized and wounded as Chris lead us to believe? It was a real turn-off."

| Case Two | A coach is not necessarily a trainer or consultant |

Jan is a corporate coach whose client requested a problem-solving session with a multi-national team. The problem? Lack of trust!

The client also wanted to use the Enneagram, which Jan didn't know well, so Jan contacted me. I agreed to do the Enneagram portion of the session followed by Jan leading the problem-solving section. Jan did hour-long individual interviews with each of the 15 team members to find out the cause of their lack of trust. Jan also sent me the data collected to get a second opinion.

Each time I received the client data, I told Jan that the data did not make sense; it did not explain why trust was low. Jan did two more complete rounds of interviews, but each time I responded the same way. The data did not clarify anything about the trust issues.

At the actual session, the Enneagram portion went well, but the problem-solving did not.

Jan first covered the walls with the data collected. The team looked puzzled. Jan then read all the data out loud. The team went from puzzled to glazed eyes. Jan froze in front of the team, looked at me, and threw me the magic marker, saying, "You take over."

Leading the problem solving was not part of my agreed-upon role, but I stood up anyway and said, "I understand the basic issue is lack of trust, but why there is lack of trust is not clear. Please divide into three groups and discuss what you think are the causes of this team's trust issues."

Fifteen minutes later, the groups shared their conclusions. It was actually very simple. The team's lack of trust was a by-product of where different team members were geographically located and related assumptions team members made about the team and team leader. The leader was based in the US. Four of the team members were from the US, while the remaining eleven were from all over the world.

The non-US-based team members assumed the US-based team members had far greater access to the leader based on proximity. This was the cause of the distrust: presumed access and influence based on proximity to the leader.

With the clear cause now identified, the entire team recognized that none of the team members actually felt they had much access to the leader. This was because the team leader was very busy, but also an Enneagram Five. As a type Five, the leader valued everyone's autonomy, trusted their work, and didn't realize that the team members needed more contact.

Why? Because, as a Five, the leader didn't want or need the contact and connection. This need for connection was just as true for US-based team members as those outside the US. The simple solution? The team leader agreed to reach out to each team member individually every other week.

Why did Jan miss this simple cause? Why did it take so much time and cost the client so much money to accomplish nothing? It was because Jan was a coach and not a consultant.

A consultant comes with diagnostic skills and also knows the right questions to ask. Jan, with a coaching background, only asked variations on questions like these: "What's going well; What's not; What needs changing?" These questions give information, but they are not diagnostic in terms of why the low trust. The simple question to ask? "What is the cause of the low trust level in this team?"

CASE THREE	A trainer is not necessarily a consultant

Blake, a well-known, experienced Enneagram trainer, was delighted when a client called requesting a daylong basic Enneagram program. The answer was *yes*.

Although the client shared their organizational challenges, Blake was not an experienced consultant and didn't realize that a basic Enneagram program for this team would have been a disaster for the client.

The 12-person team was a start-up that was about to expand over the next six months. The two founders no longer got along. Two team members had been engaged in ongoing, unresolved conflict for several months. The organizational rumor mill reported that the organization might be purchased by a large, well-known company.

Had Blake led an Enneagram training with this team, two scenarios would have been likely: the session would have fallen flat with low engagement and participation, or, even worse, all of these uncertainties and unresolved issues would have emerged and erupted during the session with no plan for how to address them.

Fortunately for the client, they also contacted Skylar, a consultant and a trainer. Skylar immediately understood the seriousness of the client's issues and the danger of using a basic Enneagram program with this team. After Skylar explained the rationale for doing organizational work prior to an Enneagram program, the client fully agreed that a potential disaster had been averted.

In working with the Enneagram, the motto should always be this: "Do no harm; do as much good as possible."

CASE FOUR	Beware of Enneagram "experts"

"Intelligent, Inc." (not their real name) used the Enneagram in their executive coaching program. The company's senior executive team had been using a consulting firm that they trusted from their prior work on strategy development. The consulting firm had several psychologists on staff, so the company's CEO asked the consulting firm to do Enneagram typing assessments for each executive team member.

The problem? The consulting firm knew nothing about the Enneagram but assumed that, because they were psychologists, all they needed to do was to read a few Enneagram books.

Wrong! 60% of the executives ended up being typed incorrectly, although neither the psychologists nor the executives realized this had happened.

The human resources department of the company did recognize the problem and contacted me in desperation. Would I train their executive coaching staff in the Enneagram system and types, with a particular focus on how to get their mistyped executives correctly typed? And could I help them develop a strategy for doing this without offending the consulting firm or the senior executives, who thought they had been typed accurately?

Mission accomplished, but redoing type is much more challenging than getting it right the first time.

How to find an excellent Enneagram trainer or consultant

Here are some good tips! There are many people all over the world who say they can do organizational work with the Enneagram, but they really don't know how. You need to know what to ask about and what to listen for.

Ask About	Listen For
Who are their prior clients or types of projects using the Enneagram?	They should have had multiple clients, but should not give their names if they also describe the exact work they did for them.
How did they learn the Enneagram?	They should have studied the Enneagram for several years with one or more reputable teachers and not just have learned it from a book or test.
How long have they been using the Enneagram in organizations?	Best is if they have been using the Enneagram in organizations for at least three years with multiple clients.
What was their role (coach, trainer or consultant) when using the Enneagram?	Remember that you are looking for a trainer or consultant, not a coach and that the skill sets are very different.
What is their approach, both structure and content, to teaching the Enneagram?	Their structure should be clear and sound like something that would work in your organization; best not to use trainers or consultants whose primary focus is the spiritual use of the Enneagram or who use language that sounds to you too spiritually-focused or overly psychological.
What was their biggest success using the Enneagram?	They should be able to give you detailed answers, but no client names; if they don't have details, they probably didn't do it.
What was their most challenging experience using the Enneagram?	They should be able to give you detailed answers, but no client names; again, listen for the level of detail.

Let's get started with Enneagram programs

Group building, team building, and professional applications

Life is really simple, but we insist on making it complicated.

—CONFUCIUS

Tie to Brand Doc

People often use the term "team building" to refer to interactive training activities that increase interpersonal connection and cohesion. You can do "team building" activities with groups or teams, even though groups are not technically teams. You can also use applications of the Enneagram with groups or teams to increase knowledge, insights and skills. For example, use the Enneagram to increase communication, decrease unproductive conflict, create a feedback culture and more.

Whether you are doing an Enneagram-based "team building" event or an Enneagram application, the best program is simple, straightforward, and always based on your purpose for using the Enneagram in your group or team.

The best advice: Don't overcomplicate it!

Simply follow the structure below. After step five, type group discussions (assuming you have enough participants to divide into type groups), do either a "team building" exercise, an Enneagram application activity or both.

OVERVIEW OF THE SESSION AGENDA	
STEP ONE	Introduction and session purpose
STEP TWO	"Ice breaker" or "warm-up" activity
STEP THREE	Overview of the Enneagram and the nine types
STEP FOUR	Typing process
STEP FIVE	Type group discussions (only if you have enough participants to divide them into groups; if not, skip this step)
STEP SIX	Team building activity, Enneagram application(s) or both
STEP SEVEN	Ending

SESSION AGENDA DETAILS	
STEP ONE: Introduction and session purpose	Introduce the program purpose and explain why the Enneagram is so important. Introduce the trainers or consultants if they don't already know the group or team.
STEP TWO: "Ice breaker" or "warm-up" activity	Use an interactive "ice breaker" or "warm-up" activity to get people engaged and to increase "psychological safety." "Ice-breakers" are shorter and get people relaxed. "Warm-up" activities are slightly longer and involve more self-reflection.
STEP THREE: Overview of the Enneagram and the nine types	Explain the nine Enneagram types accurately and without judging any type as good, bad or better than the others. Use more than lecture in the overview – visuals, short activities, short videos, engaging stories, just as examples. Longer is not necessarily better.
STEP FOUR: Typing process	Use a typing process that stimulates participant introspection, focuses on patterns of thinking, feeling and behaving rather than just observable behavior.

STEP FIVE: Type group discussions	Participants love type group discussions, but there need to be enough participants to break into type groups. Usually, 15 people or more allow for type groups. These groups also need a great question to discuss. Why? A great question focuses the discussion and stimulates the conversation. When participants have their types accurately identified, they feel they are in a discussion group where people truly understand them, like a tribe. And if people are mistyped, it often becomes obvious to them and to the group. Follow the type group discussion with a very brief report out from each group. This heightens interest in all the types and also highlights type differences.
STEP SIX: Team building activity, Enneagram application(s) or both	Option 1: Team building activity Option 2: Enneagram application(s) to topics aligned with the program's purpose An Enneagram application only works after people have their types accurately identified. Do one application in-depth or several related applications in some logical sequence. For example, a communication application can be followed by a conflict application. A leadership application can be followed by a communication application. Option 3: Combination of team building activity and application(s)
STEP SEVEN: Ending	Do something to officially end the program so the program feels complete. This can be a comment by the group or team leader, a question for each participant to reflect on, or a closing comment from each participant.

This agenda works well whether the program is done in-person or virtually. For virtual programs, here's how:

Use breakout rooms for type groups.

Use the chat function if participants have questions or for closing comments.

Put questions or activity directions in chat so participants can refer back to these when in breakout rooms.

Remember that when you bring the Enneagram to your organization, be clear on your purpose, allow people to type themselves with excellent guidance, design your programs for the most positive outcomes, and facilitate the sessions with competence and curiosity.

Teachers open the door but you enter yourself.

—CHINESE PROVERB

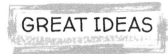

GREAT IDEAS

THE ENNEAGRAM FOR GROUP COHESION AND TEAM BUILDING

Great Idea | Enneagram "ice breakers"
These can be used whether or not participants know the Enneagram
What is your best stress reliever? How does it work?
How did you get your name?

Great Idea | Enneagram "warm-ups"
These can be used whether or not participants know the Enneagram
Think of three words that you think describe you well; write them down.
Reflect on some positive feedback you've received that really surprised you.

Great Idea | Type group discussion questions
A compelling question for each type group to answer; choose only one question and have each group answer the same question.
What do we have in common and how are we different?
Why do we think we're this type and what is one way we most often get misunderstood?

Great Idea | Team building activity
A fun, interactive and high-engagement activity that relates to the Enneagram
Enneagram Scavenger Hunt
Participants are divided into teams, with each team given a list of nine items to find, with each item representing a specific positive quality of each type. These are then shared with the large group and prizes are awarded.

Great Idea | Enneagram applications
Applications where the learning is high, the design is simple and is based on a useful concept

Motivation
Concept: people are motivated by certain factors, demotivated by others and these relate to type
Type group activity: Type groups discuss what motivates them, what demotivates them, and what they and/or their managers can do to increase their motivation.
Mixed group activity (mix up the types into groups of four-eight people): Give them the same question as above to discuss, compare answers, and explore how their answers reflect their different Enneagram types.

Go to Resources for more ideas and details.

TEAM TRANSFORMATION

From a "possible team" to a transformed, "high-performing team"

Sticks in a bundle are unbreakable.

—KENYAN PROVERB

CASEY, A CONSULTANT WHO I MENTOR, recently told me, "Ginger, I love what you say about groups versus teams. My client thinks they're a team, but I told them, 'You think you're a team but you function like a group, not like a team!' This totally got their attention, and they agreed to spend time identifying their common goals and clarifying their optimal level of interdependence. This simple concept, group versus team, made the work I did with them so much easier."

I wish I could tell you how many times I've used the concept of team versus group with my clients or with consultants and trainers that I teach. And every time I do, this simple idea – team versus group – has made a huge difference.

Most often, the conclusion is that they are a team – a possible team – although they are not acting like one.

This model shows them what to do next to become an actual team. Sometimes, they realize they are a group and not a team. This clarity usually comes with relief rather than disappointment. Better to become a great group than to try to become something which you are not.

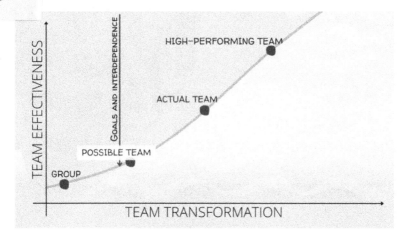

If a group recognizes they are a "possible team," then what?

Now the real fun of team transformation begins. I use a concept called AAA: alignment, attunement and acceleration. Is your team aligned and attuned so it can accelerate?

Think of this as teams being able to access the collective wisdom of their three Centers of Intelligence: Head Center, Heart Center and Body Center. Teams have all three Centers of Intelligence, just like people do. This is the challenge and opportunity for teams and individuals: *Are we accessing and using the wisdom of all three Centers of Intelligence?*

Team Alignment | the team's collective (head) mental center

Aligned teams share a mental understanding and agreement about the team's vision, goals and interdependence, as well as its operational plans. Alignment allows team members to know where they are going together and why what they're doing matters.

Think of this as the shared direction that allows a "possible team" to evolve into an "actual team."

Team Attunement | the team's collective (emotional) heart center

Attuned teams feel deeply connected to other team members' feelings and needs. They are responsive to one another and to the team as a whole because they know and care about each other. They are also passionate about the work they do together because they understand its contribution to the organization and their customers.

While alignment provides the direction, attunement fuels the energy and passion to move forward together. It's as if team members are each tuning forks keenly tuned to one another. Some refer to this as team resonance, like tuning forks working together in harmony.

Team Acceleration | the team's collective (action) body center

Accelerating teams move forward together in a common direction because they are aligned and with passion and energy because they are attuned. They know what they are doing and why.

If one team member becomes ill or over-burdened, the others not only show concern, they also step up to make sure all the work is done. No one has to ask them to do this. They just want to.

Unaligned or unattuned teams do not accelerate

Teams that are aligned but not attuned are focused and may be productive, but are not usually agile or flexible. Over time, team members feel less than their full selves at work and experience burnout quickly. They may even say they feel used by the organization.

Teams that are attuned but not aligned enjoy one another, but their collective productivity is low because their task focus is unclear. They often say they like the team and organization, but not the work itself.

Teams that are not aligned or attuned experience low productivity and low morale. They also have low trust levels and have difficulty retaining team members or recruiting new ones. Crises become everyday occurrences, and team leaders are constantly putting out fires.

These teams are simply lacking an orientation and commitment to the team's work and to each other. Would you want to work on a team like this?

Where to start with your team

You have to start with alignment and attunement at the first stage of team transformation: *Forming*. Teams need to go through four specific developmental stages on their way to becoming high-performing teams: *Forming, Storming, Norming* and *Performing*.

New teams always begin at the *Forming* stage, while older teams may be at any of the four stages.

The beauty of this developmental model is that it describes both the task (alignment) and relationship-process (attunement) challenges that need to get addressed to move to the next stage. And when these issues get identified and resolved effectively, the team becomes more aligned and more attuned, well on their way to team acceleration (action).

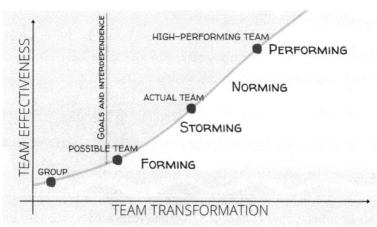

Forming stage

Think of the *Forming* stage as an orientation to both the work of the team and the people on the team. The question is what are we supposed to be doing and who are we? If the alignment and attunement *Forming* challenges are not fully addressed, the team may think it is progressing forward to action, but the unresolved issues inevitably appear as obstacles at a later stage.

These are the *Forming* challenges that need to be addressed and resolved:

Alignment challenges (task)
What is our purpose, goals, deliverables and ways of working together?

Attunement challenges (relationships and processes)
Who are we, both as individuals and as a team, and are we all included as team members?

Storming stage

As a team works together, issues arise, but do they get discussed and resolved? Resolving tensions, differences and conflict contribute to the team's forward momentum.

If these issues are not addressed, a team will struggle to move forward and will need to face them later or they will never become high-performing. Rather than accelerating, the team may even go in reverse, going back and even getting stuck in a prior stage.

These are the *Storming* challenges that need to be addressed and resolved:

Alignment challenges (task)
Are we all in agreement about where we're going and how we're getting there?

Attunement challenges (relationships and processes)
Are we bringing up and resolving areas of disagreement in a constructive way?

Norming stage

Norms are agreements about expectations and agreements about how people will behave. The *Norming* stage allows teams to reach new agreements about how they will become more aligned and attuned as a team.

Agreements about unresolved issues at the *Forming* stage get addressed at this stage, plus areas of disagreement and conflict from the *Storming* stage, as well as other issues that had not previously been identified.

These are the *Norming* challenges that need to be addressed and resolved:

Alignment challenges (task)
What agreements can we reach about how to operate more efficiently and effectively?

Attunement challenges (relationships and processes)
Are we using the most effective communication, problem-solving and decision-making skills?

Performing stage

Once teams have successfully reached agreements from the *Norming* stage, they put these new ways of working together into practice. In a sense, they test these new ways of functioning to see if they get the desired result. If not, the team simply revisits the norms and makes adjustments.

Performing is the stage all teams want to achieve. At this stage, the team is aligned, attuned and accelerating.

These are the *Performing* challenges that need to be addressed and resolved:

Alignment challenges (task)
Are we putting our customer first as we continuously learn and grow as individuals and as a team?

Attunement challenges (relationships and processes)
Are we agile, resilient and deeply supportive of each other, while also making sure we do not experience "burnout"?

How do you know the team's stage of development?

This is a crucial question because how you help the team transform depends on its current stage. The answer to this question is simpler than it might seem.

Here are two answers:

Ask the team
Share the Stages of Team Development Model with them. Then, ask the team to assess which stage they think they are at and why. Sometimes everyone agrees and sometimes not. However, their reasons for thinking that the team is at a certain stage, even if they don't agree, reveal what issues have and have not been dealt with.

For example, if some team members say *Forming* and others say *Storming*, address the *Forming* issues they identify first. These unresolved *Forming* issues will then help them all move to the *Storming* stage. The point of using the model is to help the team clarify and resolve their issues so they can make progress.

Observe their patterns of team behavior

You can also get a strong sense of the team's developmental stage by examining their observable behavior. Here's what to look for:

Forming behavior

Look for these as indicators of the *Forming* stage issues:

Engage in polite interactions but not deep ones
Act guarded and careful with each other
Ask numerous questions about what they should be doing
Rarely express disagreements
Act dependent on leader for guidance, direction, problem-solving and resolving issues
Share limited information about themselves

How can you trust anyone who doesn't know how to blush?

—CUBAN PROVERB

Storming behavior

Look for these as indicators of the *Storming* stage issues:

Passivity or conforming individual behavior, as well as avoiding each other
Aggressive, argumentative conversations, posturing for position or dominance
Don't listen to each other and interrupt one another
Ignore or act aggressively toward the leader
Sub-groups form that discuss issues privately and/or scapegoat other team members
Non-productive competition among team members

A person with too much ambition cannot sleep in peace.

—CHADIAN PROVERB

Norming behavior

Look for these as indicators of the *Norming* stage issues:

Most important issues not brought up for discussion
Topics discussed, but with no resolution or no commitment to agreements
Lack of participation or engagement from all team members in conversations
Frustrations, irritations expressed verbally and non-verbally, with no resolution
Overreliance on leader to determine working agreements instead of involving team members
Impatience with discussions taking too long

In the moment of crisis, the wise build bridges, and the foolish build dams.

—AFRICAN PROVERB

Performing behavior

Look for these as indicators of the *Performing* stage issues:

Team focuses on customer satisfaction as much or more than own satisfaction
Leader is no longer highly involved in smaller operational details and decision making
Team and individual successes celebrated on a regular basis
Team is resilient when faced with moderate or major changes
Team members know how to manage themselves and the team so they don't get "burned out"
Unresolved issues from earlier stages of development get resolved easily

It is a fact that in the right formation, the lifting power of many wings can achieve twice the distance of any bird flying alone.

—AUTHOR UNKNOWN

CHAPTER 6

FORMING STAGE

A little impatience will spoil great plans.

—CHINESE PROVERB

JAN'S NEWLY FORMED PROJECT TEAM set right to work. The eight team members were highly competent and committed to solving a crucial organizational problem related to vendors: most of their suppliers were no longer meeting their delivery deadlines due to the global pandemic. A clear task and a capable team, yet they floundered from the very start.

Their team discussions kept recycling ideas about the problem, but they could not agree on even a single solution. The reason was that the team never fully formed as a team. While they were clear about the team task, they spent no time getting to know one another as human beings or to coalesce around how they would function effectively together.

I've consulted with more than 500 teams over a 40-year time period, and this has been their biggest challenge: impatience. Teams get so focused on their tasks and what they are expected to accomplish that they get impatient with anything they think gets in the way of the work.

In other words, most teams want to jump directly to high-performing. This never works because they have skipped all the important stages that would help them get there.

Sometimes you have to go slow to go fast.

Add to this that most teams get rewarded for delivering a result, so that becomes their focus. As a result, they skip over the alignment and attunement challenges in the *Forming* stage and try to go directly to action.

In addition, people often don't know exactly how to develop stronger team relationships even if they like working on a team where people get along well toward a common mission. They may hope team relationships are positive, but view this as something that either happens naturally or it doesn't. They may believe that strong team relationships emerge only after the team has worked together over time.

The truth is that good team relationships need to start at the beginning rather than wait until the end.

If team attunement falters at the beginning, it is likely to get worse over time, not better. This orientation to speed and action, combined with not paying enough attention to team relationships, creates unaligned and non-attuned teams that will then have bigger challenges later on as they try to accelerate into high performance.

You can read some recommendations – What to do – that help you transform your teams at the very start, the *Forming* stage of team transformation.

Forming stage

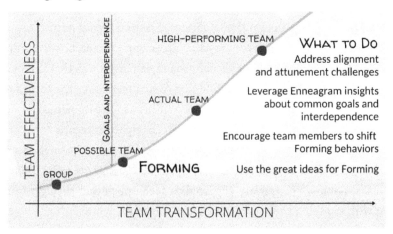

WHAT TO DO

Recommendation 1

Have a team conversation about each of these *Forming* challenges. It may take you one meeting or several, but make sure to address all the alignment and attunement issues.

Forming alignment challenges (task)

▶	Are we all clear about our team's purpose and direction?
▶	What are our common goals and expected deliverables?
▶	Do we have all the resources needed to do our work well?
▶	Do we all understand the ways in which we need to depend on each other to accomplish our work (interdependence)?

Forming attunement challenges (relationships and processes)

▶	Have we spent the time to get to know one another as people?
▶	What are the strengths that each team member brings to the team?
▶	Are we creating a culture where every team member feels included and valued?
▶	Is the "price of team membership" one that all team members are willing to pay?

The "price of team membership" refers to the implicit or explicit expectations that all team members need to meet if they want to be "full" members of the team. "Full" membership means they are taken seriously, their ideas are listened to, they feel included in team conversations, they feel respected, and they have a voice in making team decisions.

However, for some team members, the "price of team membership" may be too high. For example, the price may be having to work 60 hours weekly even though the stated expectation is 40 hours per week. For team members who need more time away from work, this price is too high. As another example, I consulted to a team where the "price of team membership" was that at the start of every monthly staff meeting, each person had to share extensive personal information. Team members who were reluctant to do this had less influence on the team.

Recommendation 2
Leverage Enneagram insights about preferred common goals and levels of interdependence

We all have Enneagram type-based preferences for the kinds of goals we prefer and the levels of interdependence we like when we work on teams. What's interesting about this is that each type-based preference has value.

This information also helps formulate team goals and get team members to support the work-required interdependencies.

Enneagram insights
Goals and interdependence preferences by Enneagram type
What kind of goals do you like?

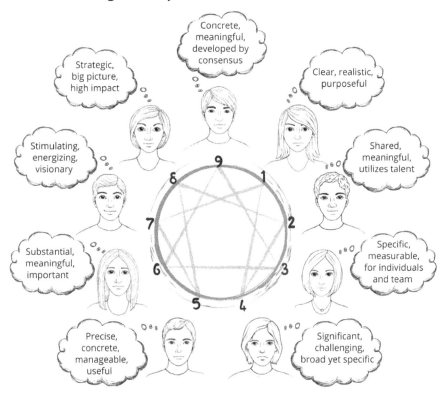

How to work with team goals

Look at what kinds of goals people of each type prefer. Although there are differences, there are also similarities. What they have in common is what matters.

So when your team formulates its goals, remember:

All nine types like team goals because team goals focus everyone's work and help everyone feel connected to each other and their team's purpose.

Most types like goals that have purpose, meaning and importance. Create your team goals making sure the bigger purpose and impact of each goal is clear to everyone.

Many types like goals that are concrete and precise enough so they know what to do. Create your team goals with this level of clarity and specificity.

"It's raining goals"

I said *no* when my long-term client, Dylan, asked if I would facilitate a goal planning session for a 12-person information technology leadership team. As an Enneagram type Seven who loves possibility and abhors limitations, Dylan hates the word *no*. Dylan had also never heard me say no in the six years we'd worked together.

Why did I say no? The team had submitted 137 goals, with another 35 coming soon. Dylan wanted me to help them prioritize their goals for the upcoming year.

I told Dylan, "You don't have a goal prioritization problem - you have a strategy problem. Many of these goals are individual ones, some are tactics, and 137 goals are impossible for your team to take action on. If you have an agreed-upon strategy, then your common team goals, one to three goals for each strategy, will be easy to use to accelerate into clear action."

Although Dylan didn't like my answer, we agreed to start with strategy and then move to goals. Dylan was elated by the result.

It turned out, as I predicted, that what they actually had among their over 100 goals was a combination of team goals, sub-team common goals, individual goals and goals for specific tasks. With their now clear strategy and manageable goals, this team was able to flourish.

What level of team interdependence do you like?

Enneagram Ones
Unambiguous interdependencies with team members who are competent and responsible

Enneagram Twos
Moderate to high interdependence as long as the team is warm, supportive and moving forward

Enneagram Threes
Clear lines of interdependence that are appropriate to the task, with focused and capable team members

Enneagram Fours
Interdependence at any level as long as it allows for self-expression and creativity

Enneagram Fives
Low interdependence that allows a high degree of autonomy with capable and efficient team members

Enneagram Sixes
Moderate to high interdependence in a like-minded, capable and loyal team

Enneagram Sevens
Fluid roles and interdependence in a democratic, stimulating and innovative environment

Enneagram Eights
Interconnectedness in an enjoyable and effective team environment where members have their own territory

Enneagram Nines
Interdependence at any level as long tasks are specific and the environment is stable with minimal tension

How to work with team interdependence

As you can read, each Enneagram type prefers different levels of interdependence in particular kinds of team environments. The good news is this: People, no matter what their type, are willing to forgo their own interdependence preferences if they understand why the required interdependence level supports the actual work of the team as a whole.

In addition to identifying the optimal level of interdependence for your team, make sure you use technology platforms that support that level of interdependence.

For example, a thirty-person team in a manufacturing company was made up of three smaller teams. For the team as a whole, low interdependence was their optimal level. But the three smaller teams required a moderate level of interdependence within each team to be effective. The technology platform they used to communicate and coordinate their work was one where all team members received every single communication.

This technology platform would have been ideal if the whole team needed to be highly interdependent, but they were not. The impact was that team members were confused about what they were supposed to know about, what they were expected to take action on and more. As a result of their chosen technology platform, this team became highly inefficient and, as a result, ineffective.

You can also use the team conversation about optimal team interdependence to create a team culture that has these characteristics:

A team where members are competent and responsible

A team culture that supports creativity and innovation

Team leadership that provides clarity of direction, but where people do not feel micromanaged

"Interdependence hubs"

A small research and development team thought their optimal interdependence level was their current one: low. Each of the six team members reasoned that they worked on completely separate research projects, so their only interdependence was with Cameron, the team coordinator. It was Cameron's role to coordinate work schedules, collect and review each person's work, and then send the work to the team leader.

As their consultant, I wondered if this way of functioning was actually their optimal level of interdependence, so I suggested we demonstrate their interdependence in a physical way.

First, they stood in a circle. I gave each person a pencil to hold; I had a ball of string. The process was this: I gave one team member the ball of string; they had to tightly wrap some string around their pencil and then throw the ball to another team member on whom they were interdependent. As they threw the ball of string, they also named the exact interdependency. The person receiving the ball of string would follow the same process. After 20 minutes, the string-based web of interdependencies was remarkable. There were so many strings around Cameron's pencil, the pencil actually broke from the strain.

It was clear that, although Cameron was the "hub" holding everything together, this was not a sustainable way of working for Cameron or the team. Would Cameron get burned out? What if Cameron took a vacation or became ill? Cameron was also an Enneagram type Five, a person who values competence, but can feel overwhelmed by too many demands and also needs time for recharging energy. In this fast-paced team, there was no time to recharge the "hub."

The team realized that if they communicated and coordinated more among themselves, they would not overload one person and their work product quality would be higher because they could learn more from each other. Drew, the team leader, realized the need to be more involved with the team members on an ongoing basis to provide support and address questions early on.

The result? This team moved from too low an interdependence to the more optimal moderate interdependence.

Enneagram insights
Forming stage behavior by Enneagram type

Here are the typical *Forming* behaviors of each Enneagram type, followed by how each can change behavior to support forward team development (indicated by the + sign).

Enneagram One typical Forming behavior

Assert opinions about the right way to structure work; more task than relationship-focused; minimal need for social connectedness

+ Value relationships and tasks equally; inquire more and advocate less; suggest ways to get to know each other better

Enneagram Two typical Forming behavior

Facilitate team discussion around core purpose; encourage people's contributions

+ Share your own thoughts more; help team reach consensus about forward movement

Enneagram Three typical Forming behavior

Assert yourself in terms of team goals and plans; want respect from the team

+ Focus on team members getting to know each other; pay less attention to how you are perceived

Enneagram Four typical Forming behavior

Focus more on internal feelings and reactions than the team task

+ Solicit the reactions of others; suggest ways to improve team functioning

Enneagram Five typical Forming behavior

Focus strongly on team goals; will engage in social connection but not for too long

+ Focus on relationships as much as tasks; share more of yourself

Enneagram Six typical Forming behavior

Prefer observing team dynamics; ask questions to clarify issues; encourage others to participate

+ Make statements about issues and how to proceed; help others get to know each other better

Enneagram Seven typical Forming behavior

Contribute multiple ideas; dislike too much structure; impatient with lack of progress

+ Listen more fully to others; embrace more structure than you prefer

Enneagram Eight typical Forming behavior

Assert directions for team; may sit back and watch, decide whether to be part of the team

+ Work more collaboratively with whole team to establish common direction; support everyone getting to know each other better

Enneagram Nine typical Forming behavior
Encourage and facilitate participation; difficulty with slow progress

+ Work hard to maintain your focus, especially when tensions arise or progress seems slow

How to work with Enneagram type behavior at the Forming stage

You can see that almost all of the Enneagram types focus more on the *Forming* tasks (alignment issues) than on relationships and processes (attunement issues). However, even the alignment challenges are often met with impatience because people want to move forward quickly. When this happens, the team will never fully form and then get stuck at the *Forming*, *Storming*, *Norming* or even the *Performing* stage.

Discuss the Stages of Team Development Model with the team, highlighting the importance of going through all four stages sequentially.

Have team members learn about and assess their own type's typical behavior at the *Forming* stage.

Have team members review and discuss the behavior change (noted by + sign) for their type and agree to experiment with these changes.

If small holes aren't fixed, then big holes will bring hardship.

—CHINESE PROVERB

GREAT IDEAS

FORMING STAGE

Great Idea | Discuss alignment and attunement issues

After the team understands the Stages of Team Development Model, designate one team member to facilitate the discussion about *Forming* alignment issues and another person to facilitate the discussion about *Forming* attunement issues.

Great Idea | Discuss Forming stage behaviors

Use "Stages of Team Development" (hard copy) tool or "Teams" (virtual) tool for each participant as a way to jump-start the conversation. These are available through TheEnneagraminBusiness.com.

Great Idea | Reward Forming stage behavior changes

Every time a team member effectively engages in the behavior change at the *Forming* stage for their type, keep a chart and give rewards for things such as these: most changes made, biggest positive impact on the team, hardest to change but at least tried, and other behaviors the team wants to acknowledge.

STORMING STAGE

Smooth seas do not make skillful sailors.

—AFRICAN PROVERB

WHAT DO TEAMS FIGHT ABOUT, and what's a fight anyway?

Denny's team stormed about what time their team meetings should start. Sam's team stormed about team members missing meetings. Reese's team complained about the workload being uneven. Kelly's team had unresolved tensions about who had more influence on the team and who had less. Dale's team had issues related to diversity and inclusion. Jamie's team knew they were not working well together, yet had no idea why.

It is not unusual for teams to not be functioning well and to not understand why. It is also common for teams to think they know what they are *Storming* about, yet be unaware that the real issues lie below the surface. For example, they may think they are *Storming* about time demands, but the real issue is feeling disrespected.

A really good analogy for this is a couple who is not getting along so they go to a couple's counselor to help them identify and resolve their issues. Sometimes the couple discovers it is how they communicate with each other, no matter what the issue. Does each person feel seen and heard? Sometimes the couple doesn't have effective problem-solving skills, so the counselor helps them learn these new ways of relating. Sometimes the couple is arguing over something small that represents something much larger.

Years ago, I went to a couple's counselor with my then partner, and the topic of disagreement was toothpaste. My partner complained that I squeezed the toothpaste tube from the middle, and it should be rolled up from the bottom. We looked to the counselor to resolve our issue, but the counselor said this: "Couples can fight about things that are not really the issue; yours is toothpaste!" Teams can be like this, too.

How explicit does the *Storming* need to be to actually be a storm? There are many answers to this question. Some teams display a great deal of overt *Storming*. Other teams appear to have almost no disagreements when they actually do. They simply don't acknowledge or discuss them. Still, other teams have only a few disagreements, yet they know what they are, and they resolve them quickly and effectively.

In addition, issues from the *Forming* stage that were not addressed often need to be dealt with at the *Storming* stage. For example, issues of diversity, equity, and inclusion that emerged, but were not effectively discussed at the *Forming* Stage, need to be addressed constructively at the *Storming* stage.

Does everyone, regardless of generation, feel equally included as full team members? Do team members from Gen Z feel minimized? Do baby boomers feel discarded? Do women feel comfortable expressing themselves? What about team members of different racial backgrounds and various gender identities and sexual orientations? Consider the experience of new team members versus longer-term team members – sometimes called the "Old Guard"? Are there inclusion issues related to geography or culture?

When addressing and moving effectively through the *Storming* stage, here are some things to remember:

All teams experience some version of *Storming*, from mild to severe.
To transform into high-performing teams, all teams need to address their particular *Storming* issues.
Too much expressed but unresolved conflict erodes team psychological safety and trust.
Too much unexpressed and unaddressed conflict typically goes underground and creates an environment of scapegoating, subgrouping that becomes unaligned with the team as a whole, rumor mills and more.
Unresolved *Storming* issues don't go away and will disable the team from moving to full high performance.
Teams that don't learn how to navigate the sometimes turbulent waters of *Storming* will not develop the skills to handle bigger issues that arise later on.

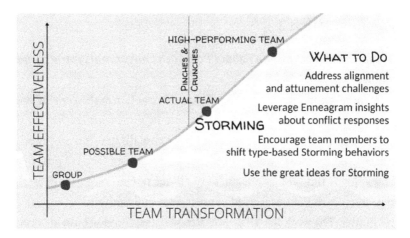

WHAT TO DO

Recommendation 1

Address the team's alignment and attunement challenges

Have a team conversation about each of these *Storming* challenges. It may take you one meeting or several, but make sure to address all the alignment and attunement issues.

Storming alignment challenges (task)

▶	Are we going in the right direction?
▶	Are we organized in a way that supports rather than impedes our work together?
▶	Are we both effective and efficient in how we operate?
▶	Do we have consensus about how well we function as a team?

Storming attunement challenges (relationships and processes)

▶	Are we willing to bring up areas of difference on issues big and small?
▶	Does everyone have a voice and are they listened to?
▶	Do we have effective conflict resolution skills?
▶	Is the team leader operating with a leadership style that supports the team's efforts?

As a note, team leaders who are conflict-avoidant often communicate that it is not OK to disagree or bring up difficult issues. They don't realize how this approach hinders the team's forward progress.

Recommendation 2

Leverage Enneagram insights about how each Enneagram type responds to conflict

Team members not only want to speed forward to action at the *Forming* stage, most team members also are uncomfortable dealing with conflict in the *Storming* stage. When conflict, whether big or small, does not get productively resolved, the team will be hindered from moving forward effectively. Yes, they might function as a team, but will not transform into high performance. Even worse, if unresolved conflict goes underground, the group dynamics suffer. The workplace becomes stressful, trust erodes, bullying occurs, leaders become delegitimized, productivity declines and worse.

Enneagram insights
Conflict and Enneagram types

Be aware, look for signals, ask the right questions. Previous Page

How do I feel about anger?

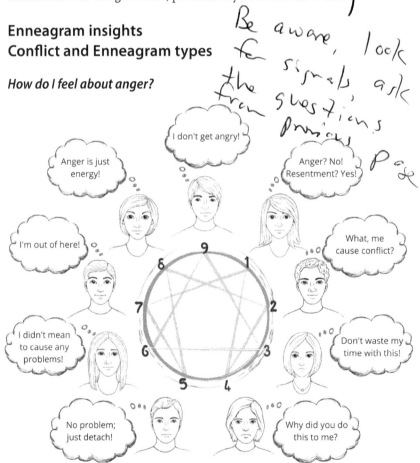

How to work with conflict

Who likes conflict? No one! Who deals with conflict productively? When people are able to manage and resolve conflict well, it is usually a learned skill.

Most of us would rather completely avoid tension and conflict or make it go away as quickly as possible. None of these reactions support a team moving effectively through the *Storming* stage. You can see the basic type-based reactions to conflict in the "How do I feel about anger" illustration.

Here are some ideas to remember:

Almost everyone is uncomfortable with conflict, even if they say this is not the case.

Conflict takes many forms, from differences of opinion and preferences to outright hostility.

When conflict is present but not addressed, it goes underground and can get really ugly; conflict that is out in the open but unresolved erodes psychological safety within the team.

What does it mean to be a team player?

Morgan, an Enneagram Six, and Quinn, an Enneagram Five, did not get along at all. Everyone on their customer service team could feel the tension between them, but no one knew why they made sharp-tongued comments to one another during team meetings or otherwise ignored each other whenever possible. With the fight between Morgan and Quinn, this team was clearly at the *Storming* stage.

At first, Morgan and Quinn couldn't say or wouldn't say what the problem was. Eventually, the issue became clear.

From Morgan's point of view as a type Six, Quinn was not acting like a team player. Quinn was not volunteering for extra assignments, was coming to team meetings on time, but never early, and was leaving directly after the meeting was over. These were the reasons Morgan firmly believed Quinn was not a loyal team player.

Quinn's perspective was very different. For Quinn as a Five, being a loyal team player meant doing your job well, delivering your work product on time, and attending team meetings as scheduled. Because Quinn was doing all these things, Quinn felt attacked and angry; Morgan felt Quinn dismissed the issues.

The Enneagram helped them resolve their conflict because it changed their perspectives. They had very different expectations of what it means to be a team player. This difference was based on their Enneagram types.

As a Six, Morgan wanted all team members to volunteer for new tasks that arose, coming early and staying late to team meetings to talk and bond. For Morgan, this created trust and safety.

As a Five, Quinn wanted all team members to do their work really well and deliver on time. For Quinn, this created trust. But having to spend more time than needed at team meetings or volunteering for extra work when others were perfectly willing to do so did not create trust. It created exhaustion and depletion.

It took the Enneagram to help Morgan and Quinn realize that their conflict about what it means to be a team player was not personal. It was based on their own type-based definitions and needs. This understanding decreased the tension between them and gave each the opportunity to engage in self-reflection and important self-development.

Enneagram insights
Storming stage behavior by Enneagram type

Here are the typical *Storming* behaviors of each Enneagram type, followed by how each can change behavior to support forward team development (indicated by the + sign).

Enneagram One typical Storming behavior

Frame conflict as a practical problem to solve; assert leadership to do this; get impatient with a prolonged emotional process

+ Be more patient with conflict discussions; encourage yourself and others to share feelings and thoughts constructively

Enneagram Two typical Storming behavior

Assist others to express thoughts and feelings toward a quick resolution; may give advice to team members

+ Encourage the conflict conversation to last until each issue gets resolved; be sure to share your own thoughts and feelings

Enneagram Three typical Storming behavior

Become disengaged; perceive conflict resolution as a waste of time or too emotional

+ Don't get frustrated because you want to move toward the work itself; encourage everyone, including you, to share their feelings

Enneagram Four typical Storming behavior

Enjoy the realness of explicit conflict as long as it doesn't get too personal or attacking and you are not the main participant in the conflict

+ Help everyone explore the deeper issues underlying the conflicts in a constructive way

Enneagram Five typical Storming behavior

Prefer to skip this stage, perceiving it as too emotional and draining

+ Become more relaxed with conflict by becoming more comfortable with your own feelings; encourage others to share in a productive way

Enneagram Six typical Storming behavior

May engage directly in conflict if improper use of authority is involved; may also feel anxious and withdraw

+ Neither over-engage nor withdraw; stay calm and listen to others; share your own perspectives

Enneagram Seven typical Storming behavior

Dislike conflict perceiving it as negative and petty; use humor to defuse tensions

+ Become more comfortable with conflict; refrain from telling jokes or stories to lighten the conversation

Enneagram Eight typical Storming behavior

Value the intensity of conflict as long as issues feel real and people are honest; if not directly part of the conflict, will facilitate resolution

+ Maintain your ability to help teams deal with conflict directly, yet respectfully

Enneagram Nine typical Storming behavior
Very uncomfortable with conflict; will try to mediate if possible; if not, will withdraw
+ Become more at ease with conflict, even when tensions are high; share your own feelings and thoughts

How to work with Enneagram type behavior at the Storming stage

You can see that almost all of the Enneagram types do not like the *Storming* stage, even if some of the types do have skills that are useful at this stage.

For example, Twos like to encourage team members to express themselves; Fours like to assist others in expressing their true feelings; Eights value the importance of dealing directly with issues; and Nines are often good mediators who encourage others to speak and then listen closely to bridge differences. That does not mean these four types, or anyone else, like conflict.

In addition, the team dynamics may be so intense and the conflict so explicit that team members of all types may withdraw from the conversations that are needed. At the other extreme, the conflict may be so unexpressed that team members can feel the tension and lack of trust, but don't know the cause or exactly how to deal with it more openly.

> Review the Stages of Team Development Model with the team, focusing on the central role of going through the *Storming* stage effectively as a key path toward transforming the team into high performance.

> Have team members learn about and assess their own type's typical behavior at the *Storming* stage.

> Have team members review and discuss the behavior change (noted by + sign) for their type and agree to experiment with these changes.

Recommendation 3
Use the Pinch-Crunch Conflict Model

The Pinch-Crunch Conflict Model is incredibly useful in describing the cycle of all relationships, at home and at work. It helps teams resolve conflicts and also has team members take responsibility for their own "hot buttons" or "pinches." It encourages team members to approach each other early to have constructive conversations.

Our "pinches" are often related to our Enneagram types, so the Enneagram is especially useful when combined with this model.

Pinch-Crunch Conflict Model

Share w/ your teams!

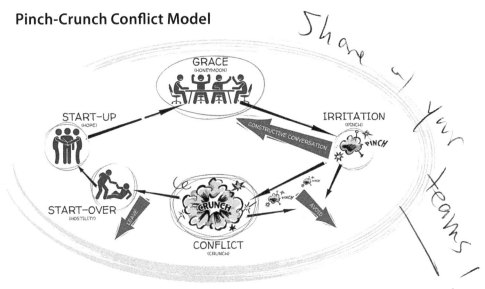

Start-Up (hope)

Most team relationships begin with a degree of hope for the future and goodwill on the part of the team members. This is the best time to share expectations with each other, including the areas in which "pinches" may occur. Unfortunately, these conversations rarely happen.

Grace (honeymoon)

"Pinches" do not typically occur in the first part of new team relationships because, during the initial encounters with others, everyone is trying to create a good impression and to get accustomed to each other and the work. Both the Start-up and Grace periods occur during the *Forming* stage of team development.

Irritation (pinch)

— let's all act immediately at "Pinch"

Over time, however, minor disruptions or "pinches" invariably occur because one person offends or irritates another. These "pinches" are often connected to our Enneagram types.

These triggers, or "pinches," occur when one person, often unknowingly, violates another person's expectations. "Pinches," which are typically knots in the stomach, can also be small jolts in the head or pangs in the chest. Along with the pinching sensation or irritation comes a thought. An internal voice says, "This person should not have done that!" along with a feeling of anger, hurt or fear.

Every "pinch" is really an early warning sign in a relationship.

When we feel a "pinch," most of us don't say anything to the other person directly. We either hope the other person's behavior is a one-time occurrence, or we speculate that the sharing of our displeasure will only make the situation worse. We think it may either create a conflict or hurt the other person's feelings.

However, it is important to say something about the "pinch" soon after it occurs so these irritations do not fester and build. The Irritation period generally occurs at the start of the *Storming* stage of team development, although "pinches" can occur during the *Forming* stage.

Conflict (crunch)

As "pinches" accumulate, they change into a conflict reaction, which is a "crunch."

During the "crunch," our feelings become more intense, our sensitivities become heightened, and the risks inherent in a discussion intensify. While it usually takes three "pinches" to create a "crunch," sometimes it only takes one or two.

When "pinches" are not addressed early, they are far more likely to become major disruptions in how the team functions later on. When expectations and "pinches" are discussed, team members have more choice and control over how they react and respond when "pinches" arise.

In addition, when conflict resolution is left until the problem has escalated to the "crunch" stage, emotions and tensions are higher, more issues have built upon one another, and the situation becomes more stressful and more risky to resolve.

The team is in full *Storming* mode.

Start-Over (hostility)

Unresolved conflict – conflict that is either avoided or dealt with ineffectively – usually damages the team. Trust and psychological safety deteriorate, team members may stop following their leader's directions, team members don't work together well on projects, and information sharing is impaired. Team members may quit, get fired, or become demotivated and disengaged.

During the Start-Over, it's important to discuss your expectations and "pinches" in a clear and explicit way. Understanding how our Enneagram type creates these expectations provides an objective perspective about why our expectations may be different.

Enneagram insights
Enneagram pinches and development areas
by Enneagram type

Here are the typical "pinches" for each Enneagram type, followed by how each can use their "pinches" and Enneagram insights for their own development (indicated by the + sign).

Enneagram One pinches and development areas

Mistakes and errors made by you or others; lack of follow-through; feeling criticized; non-collaborative change of plans; feeling deceived

+ Development areas: Relax the need to do things perfectly and avoid mistakes; refrain from being overly self-critical or critical of others

Enneagram Two pinches and development areas

Being taken for granted; feeling unappreciated; not being heard; others being treated badly; your actions being misinterpreted in negative ways

+ Development areas: Learn to set stronger boundaries; say "no" clearly; express feelings when they occur; find an inner sense of self-worth

Enneagram Three pinches and development areas

Being put in a position of likely failure; not looking good professionally; being blamed for the poor work of others; not receiving credit for your work

+ Development areas: Learn to "be" as well as "do"; explore feelings in real time; reflect on who you are in addition to your accomplishments

Enneagram Four typical pinches and development areas

Being ignored, slighted or rejected; not having your feelings honored; being forced to do something contrary to your values

+ Development areas: Explore how your constant comparisons to others make you feel deficient; reflect on how you separate yourself from others

Enneagram Five pinches and development areas

Others sharing your confidential information; being surprised or overwhelmed; dishonesty; out of control situations

+ Development areas: Explore emotions in real time rather than in delayed time; share more of yourself with others

Enneagram Six pinches and development areas

Pressure; uncertainty; lack of genuineness or commitment; abusive authority; lack of loyalty

+ Development areas: Learn to trust yourself; examine how you "test" others to determine if you can trust them

Enneagram Seven pinches and development areas

Feeling bored; repetitive tasks; feeling dismissed and not taken seriously; unjust criticism; limits placed on what you can do

+ Development areas: Learn to focus at will without distraction; explore your heart and the emotional arena; develop more consistent empathy

Enneagram Eight pinches and development areas

Indirectness; deception; injustice; others not taking responsibility; being blind-sided; not feeling in control; being manipulated

+ Development areas: Relax the need to feel in control and invulnerable; refrain from taking quick action; become more receptive

Enneagram Nine pinches and development areas

Disharmonious situations; chronic complainers; rudeness; people, including yourself, not being seen or heard; anger directed at you; feeling pressured to do something

+ Development areas: Access and express your anger; become more embodied so you know what you think and feel

Pinch-Crunch activity

Explain and discuss the Pinch-Crunch Conflict Model.

Have team members identify their "pinches" and discuss their "pinches," how these "pinches" are connected to their Enneagram type, and what their "pinch" indicates is an important area for their development. Team members will learn more about themselves, each other, and the kinds of things that "pinch" their teammates.

Encourage each team member to work on their own development to lessen the strength of their own "pinches." Help them understand that our "pinches" say as much or more about us than the person who "pinched" us.

In addition, encourage team members to go to one another when they feel the first "pinch," but after they have done their own self-reflection and development. This is the time when emotions are lower, the risk is reduced, and constructive conversations best happen. Agreeing to share "pinches" early on is a new norm that can help transition the team to the *Norming* stage.

The clash of ideas brings forth the spark of truth.

—AUSTRALIAN PROVERB

GREAT IDEAS

STORMING

Great Idea | Discuss alignment and attunement issues

After the team understands the Stages of Team Development Model, designate one team member to facilitate the discussion about *Storming* alignment issues and another person to facilitate the discussion about *Storming* attunement issues. Take care that the assigned team members are good facilitators and are comfortable discussing conflict.

Great Idea | Discuss Storming stage behaviors

Use "Stages of Team Development" (hard copy) tool, "Enneagram Conflict" (hard copy) tool or "Teams" (virtual) tool for each participant as a way to jump-start the conversation. These are available through TheEnneagramin-Business.com.

Great Idea | Incorporate Pinch-Crunch Conflict Model

Use the Pinch-Crunch Conflict Model and related process. The model, type-based "pinches," and more are all detailed on the hard copy training tool, "Enneagram Conflict." This is available through TheEnneagraminBusiness.com.

CHAPTER 8

NORMING
STAGE

Listening well is as powerful as talking well,
and is also as essential to true conversation.

—CHINESE PROVERB

SYDNEY'S PROJECT TEAM THOUGHT their deliverable was well on its way to being completed, but they also recognized none of the team members felt fully satisfied or truly proud of their product. They knew they could do better, and none of them really enjoyed the experience of working together. It wasn't awful, but it wasn't that good either.

When they learned the Stages of Team Development, they realized they had not gone through the *Storming* stage effectively. They had bypassed any differences that emerged and only pursued their project work. As a result of this insight, they decided to allow themselves to storm. They did this well, and after the storming conversations, they discussed new norms.

Their new norms were simple and they worked. Each time a suggestion on how to proceed came forward, they would ask each team member for their thoughts about the idea. If a team member disagreed, instead of debating the issue, the team used inquiry instead. What was the person's concern? Did they have a better idea? This worked well for the team and allowed them to become more aligned, attuned and to accelerate together.

When addressing and moving effectively through the *Norming* stage, here are some things to remember:

▶ Some, but not all, topics that are important to create norms about arise in the *Storming* stage.
▶ Teams may have already created some workable norms at the *Forming* stage and during the *Storming* stage.
▶ Make sure everyone is clear about and agrees to the new norms; otherwise, *Storming* will arise when team members don't follow the new norms.
▶ Teams need to know when to stop creating new norms because too many norms, especially those about issues that could arise but haven't yet, can create rigid rather than agile teams.

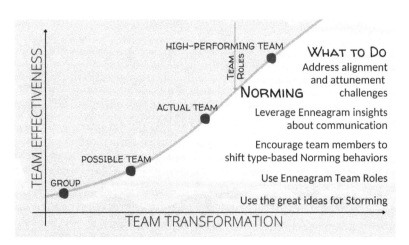

WHAT TO DO

Recommendation 1
Address the team's alignment and attunement challenges

Have a team conversation about each of these challenges. It may take you one meeting or several, but make sure to address all the alignment and attunement issues.

Norming alignment challenges (task)

What areas do we need to discuss and reach agreements about so we can operate more *effectively*?
What areas do we need to discuss and reach agreements about so we can operate more *efficiently*?
Have we created norms that resolve prior areas of conflict from the *Storming* stage?
Are there other working agreements we need to make that may seem like minor ones but are still important?

Norming attunement challenges (relationships and processes)

Are we using our communication and problem-solving skills effectively?
Are we speaking up when we have an idea or a contribution to make?
Are we fully listening to everyone?
Are we using a decision-making process that works for us?

As a note, teams make norms about very important items, such as how they coordinate their work better, but also about smaller items that also matter to them. For example, I've seen teams create new norms about lateness to team meetings or what will be served at team lunches.

Recommendation 2
Leverage Enneagram insights about communication styles

We all have type-based ways in which we communicate with others that can create misunderstandings when teams discuss new norms for their team. Understanding this information is especially relevant when discussing new ways of operating together.

What I am thinking when I communicate with others

How to work with communication styles

There are so many aspects to each type's communication style, but here you can read about the main areas different Enneagram types need to pay attention to.

Active engagement

When discussing new norms, each team member needs to actively engage in the conversation. Active engagement means they actually are contributing thoughts and feelings about what is being discussed.

Some Enneagram types may be reluctant to fully engage – for example, Fours, Fives and Nines. Fours may withdraw if they do not perceive the conversation as deep enough; Fives withdraw by not speaking very much, although they are often having an internal dialogue about what is being discussed; Nines may say something, but more often they are hesitant to share their own thoughts and feelings throughout the conversation. Encourage active participation from everyone.

Non-judgmental atmosphere

When discussing new norms, a non-judgmental, non-evaluating environment produces the best outcomes. Only after all ideas have been heard can the team make a decision that will work well and be followed. Pay special attention to the following Enneagram types who may, unintentionally, limit the conversation: Ones, Sixes and Sevens.

Ones have strong opinions, assert them quickly, and believe theirs is the correct one. Sixes regularly ask "What-if" questions after suggestions are made, which is not intended to shut down the conversation, yet can have this effect. Sevens tend to jump in with numerous ideas and so many alternative suggestions that the team may not know which of their ideas to pursue.

Relaxed pace

Keep the conversation moving at a relaxed pace – not too slow and certainly not too fast. If the team conversation moves too quickly, many people of all types are not sure when to speak up. If it goes too slowly, many team members will lose patience.

Bring closure to each item

Finally, make sure every topic that needs a norm is discussed to completion. After the discussion, ask the team if they have reached consensus before moving on to the next topic.

Recommendation 3
Norming stage behaviors and suggestions

Enneagram insights
Norming stage behavior by Enneagram type

Here are the typical *Norming* behaviors of each Enneagram type, followed by how each can change behavior to accelerate team development (indicated by the + sign).

Enneagram One typical Norming behavior
Suggest rules and standards for working better together
  + Seek consensus for your ideas; encourage others to also make suggestions

Enneagram Two typical Norming behavior
Encourage the team to make clear agreements and that everyone agrees
  + Make sure to also express your own ideas; ask other team members for their reactions

Enneagram Three typical Norming behavior
Suggest ideas; support the team being unified and focused by offering ideas and affirming practical ideas of others
  + Make sure to suggest norms related to relationships and processes as well as tasks

Enneagram Four typical Norming behavior
Suggest and support norms that add clarity as long as they don't restrict individual creativity and expression
  + Be open to ideas that may feel restrictive to you if these are in the best interests of the team moving forward

Enneagram Five typical Norming behavior
Like clear rules and boundaries as long as these allow for enough autonomy
  + Be more vocal about your ideas and support suggestions that don't allow the level of autonomy you prefer but are important for the team as a whole

Enneagram Six typical Norming behavior
Actively work to seek agreement among all team members, with attention to equal participation from everyone regarding the needs of the team
  + Also support suggestions that meet individual as well as team needs when possible

Enneagram Seven typical Norming behavior
Suggest a minimal number of rules because too many rules limit your freedom

+ Support team norms that are good for the team, even if you feel your freedom might be limited, and commit to following these

Enneagram Eight typical Norming behavior
Encourage the team to create norms, particularly ones that allow everyone to be heard because this is the fair way to move forward

+ Also make suggestions about norms; be receptive to what others say in response

Enneagram Nine typical Norming behavior
Support and facilitate norms developed by consensus, but resist norms that are not consensually developed

+ Make sure to share your own ideas; be open to suggestions you think were not developed initially with everyone's participation

How to work with Enneagram type behavior at the Norming stage

You can see that almost all of the Enneagram types do much better at the *Norming* stage than the prior two stages of team development. Each Enneagram type brings certain skills that are very helpful at this stage, yet each team member can help the team accelerate by shifting or expanding their behaviors.

Review the Stages of Team Development Model with the team, focusing on the importance of creating new ways of working together that support the team's alignment and attunement.

Have team members learn about and assess their own type's typical behavior at the *Norming* stage.

Have team members review and discuss the behavior change (noted by + sign) for their type and agree to experiment with these changes.

Recommendation 4
Stretch your team roles

Productive team conversations are essential at all stages of team development, and they are crucial when teams engage in dialogue at the *Norming* stage. Sometimes teams get stuck – think of being stuck as being in a conversational "rut" – and don't understand how to change this. Part of the reason is that team members are playing certain repetitive team roles.

These roles, a role related to the tasks of the team and the other related to team relationships and processes, grow out of our Enneagram types. Once team members recognize the roles they each play, they can enhance the conversations by shifting their roles. This can be fun to do. Even more important, it changes the process by which important conversations occur and creates far more innovative and productive outcomes.

TASK ROLES
Team-based behaviors directed toward the actual work

VS

RELATIONSHIP ROLES
Team-based behaviors focused on feelings, relationships, and team processes, such as decision making and conflict resolution

Team-based behaviors directed toward the actual work

These task team roles are all important for any team to communicate effectively.

TASK ROLES	
Structuring tasks	Making suggestions about how to organize the work
Giving opinions	Stating clear positions about items under discussion
Soliciting information	Seeking information from others related to the task about topics such as what, how, why, when and who
Defining goals	Helping articulate and clarify the team's concrete goals and deliverables
Tracking tasks	Demonstrating knowledge of how the team is progressing with regard to work and what is needed to move the task along

Managing the agenda	Commenting and influencing the team with regard to whether the important items are on the agenda, how the team is working through the agenda, and how the items are prioritized
Managing resources	Paying attention to and monitoring the team's resources, such as time, money, staffing and materials
Evaluating information	Reacting to and evaluating ideas and information presented by others
Generating and elaborating on ideas	Bringing up new ideas and providing additional input to an idea already under discussion
Defining larger purpose	Stating or helping the team clarify its charter and purpose
Giving information	Providing others with information related to the task, such as information about what, how, why, when and who

Team-based behaviors focused on feelings, relationships, and team processes, such as decision making and conflict resolution

These relationship team roles are as important as the task roles for any team to communicate effectively.

RELATIONSHIP ROLES	
Suggesting norms	Offering ideas about how the team can operate more effectively, such as ideas about timeliness, decision making, etc
Encouraging partici-pation	Soliciting (both verbally and nonverbally) everyone's participation
Facilitating to move the process ahead	Summarizing, synthesizing, probing, charting, and other behaviors designed to move the process ahead
Expressing feelings	Sharing own emotions with the team or helping others to do this
Providing perspective	Stating complex issues in a larger and more objective context so that alternative views and courses of action can be considered
Playing devil's advocate	Articulating obstacles that need to be considered or overcome
Relieving tension	Using humor or other behavior designed to reduce team tension
Challenging	Confronting, questioning, and asking direct questions or making direct statements

▶ Harmonizing team interactions	Helping people get along, feel comfortable, connect with others and achieve consensus
▶ Facilitating the positive resolution of conflict	Drawing out the feelings and perspectives of others in relation to conflict and facilitating its constructive resolution

Enneagram insights
Task and relationship roles for each Enneagram type

Each Enneagram type has typical task and relationship roles. These roles are something team members of each type play, but they are not making a conscious choice to do so. That's because these roles are natural and predictable patterns of behavior that grow from our Enneagram types.

Here are the typical task and relationship roles of each Enneagram type, followed by how each can shift behavior to expand their role and support team development (indicated by the + sign).

Enneagram One team roles
Typical task role: Structuring tasks and giving opinions
    + Task role shift: Soliciting information
Typical relationship role: Suggesting norms (working agreements)
    + Relationship role shift: Facilitating the positive resolution of conflict

Enneagram Two team roles
Typical task role: Soliciting information
    + Task role shift: Giving opinions
Typical relationship role: Encouraging participation
    + Relationship role shift: Facilitating to move the process ahead

Enneagram Three team roles
Typical task role: Defining goals and tracking tasks
    + Task role shift: Managing the agenda
Typical relationship role: Facilitating to move the process ahead
    + Relationship role shift: Encouraging participation

Enneagram Four team roles

Typical task role: Managing the agenda
+ Task role shift: Defining goals and tracking tasks
Typical relationship role: Expressing feelings
+ Relationship role shift: Providing perspective

Enneagram Five team roles

Typical task role: Managing resources
+ Task role shift: Defining larger purpose
Typical relationship role: Providing perspective
+ Relationship role shift: Expressing feelings

Enneagram Six team roles

Typical task role: Evaluating information
+ Task role shift: Generating and elaborating on ideas
Typical relationship role: Playing devil's advocate
+ Relationship role shift: Relieving tension

Enneagram Seven team roles

Task role: Generating and elaborating on ideas
+ Task role shift: Structuring tasks
Typical relationship role: Relieving tension
+ Relationship role shift: Playing devil's advocate

Enneagram Eight team roles

Typical task role: Defining larger purpose
+ Task role shift: Managing resources
Typical relationship role: Challenging
+ Relationship role shift: Harmonizing team interactions

Enneagram Nine team roles

Typical task role: Giving information
+ Task role shift: Evaluating information
Typical relationship role: Harmonizing team interactions and facilitating the positive resolution of conflict
+ Relationship role shift: Challenging

Team roles activity

Review the task and relationship roles listed as the typical ones for each team member's Enneagram type.

Have each team member reflect on these roles and how they are related to their Enneagram types.

Next, have each team member experiment with the new task and relationship team roles during a team meeting.

These roles will be very different from each person's customary roles. The most challenging roles to try are the ones most different from their typical task and relationship roles. Trying these new roles is also stimulating and energizing.

About 15-30 minutes into the conversation, have the team discuss their experience and what kind of difference this shift of roles made for their effective team functioning.

Because this activity can help change the behavior of individual members of a team, it is also a provocative and highly effective way to alter a team's interpersonal dynamics. When one person changes their behavior, the change affects the way everyone on the team behaves. When several people shift their behavior, the resulting changes in team dynamics are even more profound.

You may be wondering if team members can actually do the activity of shifting their typical task and relationship roles. The answer is an absolute yes! In the many times I have done this with teams, there was only one person who could not do it. But hundreds of others can!

The activity brings breakthrough conversations, increases team members' interpersonal agility, and is something they continue to use in team meetings.

A memorable time was with a very senior team; all members were vice-presidents or higher. Alex was a longtime team member, an Enneagram Five, and well-respected but usually said very little at team meetings. Alex was willing to occasionally share important ideas but never feelings.

However, when Alex participated in these new roles – defining the larger purpose and expressing feelings – Alex shared feelings clearly, honestly and with great insight. After the shock of hearing such deep emotions from someone who never shared any, the team asked, "Was this hard for you?" Alex's answer was profound and got everyone's attention. "No one ever asked. My feelings were in there all the time."

Without standards, no boundaries are set.

—CHINESE PROVERB

GREAT IDEAS

NORMING

Great Idea | Discuss alignment and attunement issues
After the team understands the Stages of Team Development Model, designate one team member to facilitate the discussion about *Norming* alignment issues and another person to facilitate the discussion about *Norming* attunement issues. Take care that the assigned team members are good facilitators.

Great Idea | Discuss Norming stage behaviors
Use "Stages of Team Development" (hard copy) tool, "Team Roles" (hard copy) tool or "Teams" (virtual) tool for each participant as a way to jump-start the conversation. These are available through TheEnneagramInBusiness.com.

Great Idea | Practice new team roles
Use the Team Roles Model and related process. Encourage team members to keep practicing their new roles and then experiment with trying other roles as well.

CHAPTER 9

PERFORMING STAGE

One finger cannot lift a pebble.

—HOPI PROVERB

I'VE BEEN LEADING A GLOBAL TEAM for three years to develop a global survey on the uses and value of using the Enneagram in organizations. The reason it's taken three years is simple. We were almost ready to release the survey after working on it for a year and then the Covid pandemic hit worldwide.

The team had been high-performing up to this point, although we had initially struggled through the *Storming* phase. It took us time to gain consensus on what information we were really seeking and the best way to ask questions related to this. When we stopped working together due to the pandemic, we were all disappointed, but sending out a survey of this kind during such difficult times seemed insensitive. People globally were worried about life, health and economics.

When we regrouped two years later, the team was still high-performing. Everyone wanted to continue on the team, and a few team members with special talents and expertise took the old survey and updated it to be responsive to the current environment. Other team members readily volunteered for other tasks: translation oversight, survey roll-out, graphic design and more.

It was as if we had all developed a "high-performing muscle" that stayed with us even two years later.

When addressing and moving effectively through the *Performing* stage, here are some things to remember:

> ▶ High-performing teams are agile, enthusiastic and committed.

> ▶ High-performing teams will have these characteristics: customer-focused, increasingly high levels of expertise and skills, resilience and a culture of support and development.

> ▶ Issues from the prior stages – *Forming*, *Storming* and *Norming* – may emerge during the *Performing* stage, but this doesn't mean the challenges of prior stages were not addressed. They may simply be new challenges.

> ▶ Teams that have gone through the four stages of team development effectively will be well equipped to deal with new issues that arise more constructively and will move through them more quickly.

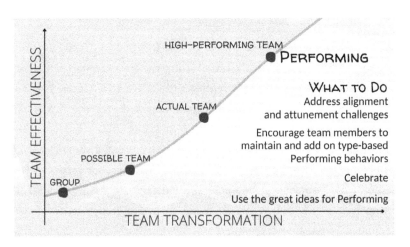

WHAT TO DO

Recommendation 1
Address the team's alignment and attunement challenges

Have a team conversation about each of these challenges. It may take you one meeting or several, but make sure to address all the alignment and attunement issues.

Performing alignment challenges (task)

▶ Is our focus on our customer first and ourselves second?
▶ Do we assess what are we doing well that we want to continue?
▶ Are there areas we want to change or improve that will help us work more effectively and efficiently?
▶ Are we learning and growing in our technical expertise and skills as a team and as individuals?

Performing attunement challenges (relationships and processes)

▶ Are we agile and resilient as a team and as individuals?
▶ Do we fully support and encourage the growth and development of each other?
▶ Do we celebrate our individual and collective successes?
▶ Do we watch out for one another and make sure we're not getting burned out?

Some teams will think they are high-performing because they do their technical work well. However, they put themselves first in terms of defining success and assume that they are serving the customer well. However, just because a team can solve complex customer problems or they enjoy their work doesn't mean they know, care or ask what the customer wants from them.

Recommendation 2
Performing stage behaviors and suggestions

Enneagram insights
Performing stage behavior by Enneagram type

Here are the typical *Performing* behaviors of each Enneagram type, followed by how each type can prevent burnout (indicated by the + sign).

Enneagram One typical Performing behavior

Embrace the high production of excellent quality

+ Take care of yourself, making sure you don't work so hard and long that you don't take time for relaxation and fun

Enneagram Two typical Performing behavior
Take great pleasure in the team's high performance, especially in support of other high-performing team members

+ Be sure to not overly volunteer to help other team members when they become overloaded, or you will become overwhelmed yourself

Enneagram Three typical Performing behavior
Relish the results at this stage and encourage everyone's top performance

+ Be careful not to work so hard for extended periods of time that you become exhausted

Enneagram Four typical Performing behavior
Feel most included in the team and work very hard on behalf of the team's goals

+ Enjoy this stage, yet be careful about doing too much work or feeling disheartened when team members leave, or the team disbands

Enneagram Five typical Performing behavior
Prefer individual tasks in areas of your competence, yet also enjoy the team's success

+ Volunteer more to help others when they are overloaded, while still respecting your own time boundaries and energy

Enneagram Six typical Performing behavior
Keep others focused on deliverables, while acting as a troubleshooter and acknowledging team member's contributions

+ Make sure to honor and acknowledge your own contributions as much as you do those of other team members

Enneagram Seven typical Performing behavior
Tend to work on own priorities as well as the team's; like roles and tasks with positive interactions

+ Make sure your priorities are so fully aligned with those of the team that you don't add extra work for yourself based on your ability to generate so many new ideas

Enneagram Eight typical Performing behavior

Fully engage when the team's productivity and products are high impact, but less so when the work seems less significant

+ Stay fully engaged, but also notice your first indicators of burnout; take care of your needs early on, don't wait until you are absolutely exhausted

Enneagram Nine typical Performing behavior

Take great satisfaction in getting something done in a harmonious team environment

+ Maintain your ability to enjoy yourself and the team without exhausting yourself because you've thrown yourself 100% into the work

How to work with Enneagram type behavior at the Performing stage

You can see that almost all of the Enneagram types naturally do much better at the *Performing* stage than the other three stages. Each Enneagram type brings certain skills that are very helpful at this stage, yet each can help the team accelerate by shifting or expanding their behaviors.

Review the Stages of Team Development Model with the team, focusing on the importance of maintaining a sustainable pace of working and allowing space for celebrating successes.

Have team members learn about and assess their own type's typical behavior at the *Performing* stage.

Have team members review and discuss the behavior change (noted by + sign) for their type and agree to experiment with these changes.

Recommendation 3
Leverage Enneagram insights about
how to plan a team celebration

We all have type-based ways we like to celebrate. Here are some type-based orientations about celebrations to consider.

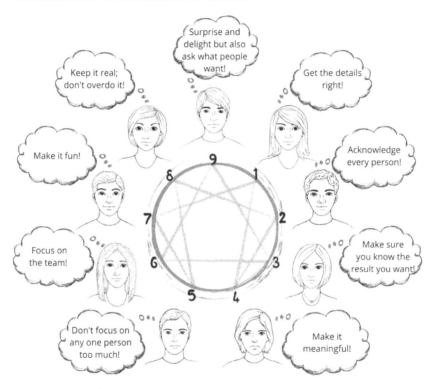

Recommendation 4
Celebrations

What to celebrate

Team milestones		
	Results-based milestones based on the completion of certain tasks or customer deliverables	
	Time-based milestones that highlight the amount of time the team's been together	
	Process-based milestones based on accomplishing certain processes such as implementing a new technology	

Birthdays and anniversaries, including work anniversaries
Different holidays
Various cultures through art, music, food or history while making sure to avoid stereotyping
Someone leaving or joining the team
Positive feedback from clients or the organization

How to celebrate

Offer sincere praise when the team or team members have done something outstanding.
Invite guest speakers.
Send handwritten notes or emails to the team and/or individuals.
Make individual phone calls.
Send small gifts or gift cards from Amazon, iTunes or other providers.
Send larger gifts such as items from SnackMagic where you can choose what to send people or send a dollar amount and they choose.

It's amazing how much people get done if they do

not worry about who gets the credit.

—SWAHILI PROVERB

GREAT IDEAS

PERFORMING

Great Idea | Discuss alignment and attunement issues

After the team understands the Stages of Team Development Model, designate one team member to facilitate the discussion about *Performing* alignment issues and another person to facilitate the discussion about *Performing* attunement issues.

Great Idea | Discuss Performing stage behaviors

Use "Stages of Team Development" (hard copy) tool or "Teams" (virtual) tool for each participant as a way to jump-start the conversation. These are available through TheEnneagraminBusiness.com.

Great Idea | Celebration planning

Get part or all of the team involved in designing the celebrations, unless it's a surprise celebration.

CHAPTER 10

TEAM MAPS

In our togetherness, castles are built.

—IRISH PROVERB

ALTHOUGH THIS STORY MAY BE HARD TO BELIEVE, it's true. I was leading a one-day Enneagram basic training for a group of 45 people following an agenda we were using throughout the entire organization: the Enneagram system, typing, communication, feedback and relationships.

At lunch, several participants approached me making this request: "Please focus some of our afternoon time on the topic of the Enneagram and teams because this group is made up of two entirely independent teams." One team had been around for two years, while the other team was brand new.

I said yes, although I had none of my team-based training materials with me. What I did have was a large Enneagram symbol on fabric, 54 by 54 square inches.

What we did stunned them.

We had the long-standing team sit at the front of the room, and we taped an Enneagram symbol map behind them on the wall. Each team member's Enneagram type was placed on this map using a large sticky dot next to their types. This long-standing team was instructed to remain silent while the newer team was taught how to "read" the map and predict how the longer-standing team had been operating based on the types shown.

Using the team mapping process, I taught them to focus first on the three Centers of Intelligence – Head, Heart and Body – shown on the map. Three types – Eight, Nine and One – are formed from the Body Center of Intelligence and share certain characteristics: action, the need to have things under control and fairness. Three other types – Two, Three and Four – are formed from the Heart Center of Intelligence and share certain characteristics: relationship orientation, concern about how others perceive them (image) and feelings. The remaining three types – Five, Six and Seven – are formed from the Head Center of Intelligence and share certain characteristics: idea generation, mental processing and planning.

The key to this analysis is to see visually which Centers might be over- and under-represented within the team because all Centers are important for effective team functioning.

With this information, the new team spent 45 minutes identifying the strengths, vulnerabilities and dynamics of the longer-standing team with, as the longer-standing team said, about 95% accuracy.

The new team was intrigued by this and asked the longer-standing team to offer insights about how they, the new team, were likely to function based on the Centers of Intelligence analysis. The new team chose to put the Enneagram symbol on the floor and stand in their type positions as the analysis began. The new team found the insights from the analysis extremely helpful and then discussed how they could leverage their strengths and make adjustments for the Centers not fully represented in the existing team.

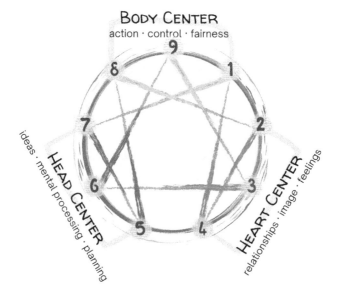

As you can see, the Enneagram can take your team beyond the powerful insights of how each Enneagram type thinks, feels and behaves. The Enneagram symbol itself is actually a map that accurately predicts the whole team's performance based on a composite of all team members' Enneagram types.

Enneagram team mapping is powerful because it does the following:

Accurately predicts the strengths and the areas of tension within a team quickly

Allows teams to view themselves objectively, recognizing strengths and areas for growth

Depersonalizes the conversation in a highly constructive way

Ignites powerful yet dispassionate dialogue to improve performance

The Enneagram mapping process | The six steps

Step 1 | Mark each team member's type on the symbol (map)
Using an Enneagram symbol, place a mark on the type number of each team member – for example, use a colored sticky dot or a magic marker. Indicate the team leader's Enneagram type using a different colored sticky dot or mark.

Step 2 | Identify visible patterns
Have team members comment on what they see on the map in terms of patterns of Enneagram types, starting first with the most heavily represented and most underrepresented Centers of Intelligence on the team. They'll likely notice other patterns as well, such as a large number of certain types and the absence of others.

Step 3 | Explain each Center of Intelligence's orientation
Remind team members that each Center has a certain orientation or emphasis – specifically, Head Center types emphasize ideas, mental processing and planning; Heart Center types emphasize relationships, image (how they are perceived) and feelings; and Body Center types focus on action, control and fairness.

Step 4 | Analyze how the team functions as reflected on the map

Have team members analyze what their Enneagram team map illuminates about how their team actually functions, particularly based on the number of team members within each Center – as a team, what they pay attention to, what they pay less attention to, and some of the areas of tension.

Note that while some teams are well balanced by Centers, most are less so. Even with teams that have all three Centers of Intelligence represented somewhat evenly, still probe whether the balance of Centers creates an effective dialogue within the team in terms of thinking, feeling and doing or whether these different emphases create tensions.

Step 5 | Reflect on how to address team strengths and limitations

After the team identifies its strengths and limitations, have them discuss how specific team members or the team as a whole can respond to the less emphasized areas.

For example, individuals can access more qualities from their wings – the types on either side of their core Enneagram type – and the types that are connected to their core Enneagram type through the lines on the Enneagram symbol. These lines are also referred to as arrow lines. As an example, there is an arrow line that connects type Three to type Nine and another that connects type Six and type Nine. Similarly, each Enneagram type has a line to and away from its number.

In addition to discussing how to use wings and arrow lines, teams can develop specific questions or areas of focus to address at every team meeting. This reminds them to pay attention to areas they may de-emphasize.

As a note of caution, if there is a heavy predominance of a certain Center or even a type within a Center, make sure to discourage teams from thinking they should simply hire more people of a missing Center or a specific Enneagram type. Hiring should be based on skills, experience and self-mastery levels. These are far better predictors of a person's effectiveness and success than is Enneagram type.

Step 6 | *Analyze team interactions based on specific type orientations*

Once teams have discussed the Centers of Intelligence represented, the conversation can move to the over- and under-representation of specific Enneagram types. Teams that understand the Enneagram system and their own types well can do this with a minimum amount of guidance from a facilitator; teams newer to the Enneagram require more guidance.

Team map examples

Here are three different team maps from real teams. Each team has a different combination of types, and the team map analysis will show you how to work with these dynamics.

What is the best way to do this with a team? Teach them the six-step team map analysis principles and have them do the analysis and discussion, followed by a discussion about what they've learned and what they can change.

Team map 1

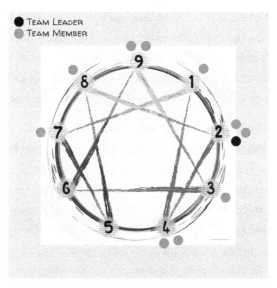

Step 1 | *Mark each team member's type on the symbol (map)*

Step 2 | *Identify visible patterns*

What's obvious is that this team has the largest number of members that are Heart Center types (Twos, Threes and Fours), including the leader, several

Body Center types (Eights, Nines and Ones), and only one Head Center type, a type Seven. There are no Fives and Sixes.

Step 3 | Explain each Center of Intelligence's orientation
Heart Center (highest) relationships, image, feelings
Body Center (second highest) action, control, fairness
Head Center (lowest) ideas, mental processing, planning

Step 4 | Analyze how the team functions as reflected on the map
As a result of the high number of Heart Center members, this team is people-focused, paying attention to team relationships and relationships with staff and customers.

With several team members in the Body center, this team is also action-oriented and likes things to be under control.

With only one Head Center team member, the team places far less emphasis on deliberation and planning.

Although the team does engage in planning, their planning is not as systematic or fact-based as it could be. For example, although they do conduct customer surveys, the questions relate almost exclusively to how customers feel about the products and services. These are Heart Center questions, not questions about what product features customers prefer (Head Center questions) or about timeliness and delivery (Body Center questions).

Step 5 | Reflect on how to address team strengths and limitations
With so many Heart Center types, this team decided it would be very helpful for certain members to raise issues related to data gathering and planning much more frequently. In addition, they would also build a far more rigorous data collection and planning process into their bi-annual goal-setting activities.

They also recognized that having only one Head Center type (type Seven) put pressure on that team member to speak out in meetings and to be fully heard. In other words, it was common that when this team member raised an idea, other team members either disagreed or ignored what was said. Had there been other Head Center team members (type Five or Six), these team members would more likely have pursued and discussed these ideas. The team agreed to listen more carefully and fully to what the type Seven team member suggested.

Step 6 | Analyze team interactions based on specific type orientations

The team discussed certain interactions - for example, that Threes and Eights are both forward moving. However, Eights like big action with large impact, and Threes like any variety of action as long as they yield results. This difference, at times, caused communication barriers within the team. They decided to move to action in both bigger and smaller ways.

Team map 2

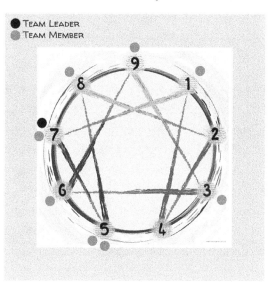

Step 1 | Mark each team member's type on the symbol (map)

Step 2 | Identify visible patterns

What's obvious is that this team has the largest number of members that are Head Center types, including the leader, several Body Center types, and only one Heart Center type, a type Three. There are no Twos or Fours.

Step 3 | Explain each Center of Intelligence's orientation

Head Center (highest) ideas, mental processing, planning
Body Center (second highest) action, control, fairness
Heart Center (lowest) relationships, image, feelings

Step 4 | *Analyze how the team functions as reflected on the map*

With so many Head Center types, this team generates an abundance of ideas – five of the nine team members, including the team leader, are Head Center types.

The team also has a moderate degree of action orientation – the team has three Body Center types. With so many ideas being generated, the team also has difficulty determining which ideas they should execute.

With so few Heart Center types, team members also pay less attention to the impact of their decisions on people or to overall morale within their business unit. As they said, "It's not the first thing we think about; it's the third, if even that."

Step 5 | *Reflect on how to address team strengths and limitations*

The first issue the team discussed was both a problem and an opportunity. They generated so many ideas, many of them good ones, but what should they take action on? The solution was simple. They agreed to take each idea, one at a time, decide whether to take action on it, and then move to the next idea.

The team also decided to pay more attention to the human aspect of the organization. Although they thought of themselves as interested in people, they had the lowest moral survey scores in the entire organization.

As a more Head Center-oriented team, this data grabbed their attention. The team agreed that every time they made any decision in the future, they would spend 10 minutes discussing the following question, one that they put on the wall in their meeting room as a reminder: *What is the impact of our decision on people, and what can we do to minimize any negative impact?*

They also realized they could not expect a single Heart Center team member, the type Three, to always raise people issues. First, it is hard to be a solo voice for this without any other Heart Center team members. Second, although Threes are Heart Center types, they may focus their Heart Center more on customer relations and how the team is perceived by other business units than on issues such as internal morale. The team decided to pay "attention by intention" to people issues both within their team and in the wider business unit.

Step 6 | Analyze team interactions based on specific type orientations

The most intriguing discussion came when they examined the types within their team and, in particular, how the Head Center types interacted when they discussed ideas.

The two Fives wanted the team to be very deliberate in evaluating the ideas generated. The Sixes had many ideas, but they also questioned the ideas of others with many "What if" questions. The Sevens, however, just loved generating ideas and possibilities and felt slowed down by the Fives and Sixes. This was accentuated by the leader being a type Seven. This leader often created the most ideas, leaving everyone else to wonder which of these ideas the leader wanted them to take action on.

Once this team dynamic became clear, the team agreed to develop specific criteria for deciding which ideas warranted action. They added these criteria to their earlier agreement to take one idea at a time.

Team map 3

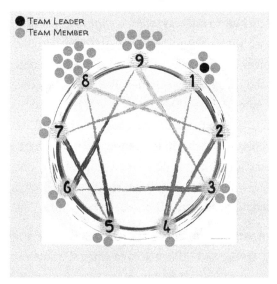

Step 1 | Mark each team member's type on the symbol (map)

Step 2 | Identify visible patterns

What's obvious is that this team has the largest number of members that are

Body Center types, including the leader, several Head types, and only a few Heart Center types.

Step 3 | Explain each Center of Intelligence's orientation
Body Center (highest) action, control, fairness
Head Center (second highest) ideas, mental processing, planning
Heart Center (lowest) relationships, image, feelings

Step 4 | Analyze how the team functions as reflected on the map
This large team has a strong representation of Body Center types, including the leader who is a One. So extreme was their action orientation that upon seeing the map, the leader said, "We're highly action-oriented. What's wrong with that?"

After further discussion, the team realized that they paid little attention to planning (Head Center orientation) and were often fighting fires rather than preventing them, all because they took action so quickly.

In addition, they placed very little emphasis on the interpersonal relationships between them or with their customers.

Step 5 | Reflect on how to address team strengths and limitations
From working with their Enneagram map, the team concluded, "We don't have time to plan, but this is because we take way too much time fixing problems that should never have occurred in the first place."

The Head Center types on the team – Fives, Sixes and Sevens – agreed to be more assertive about voicing their concerns related about taking too much action too quickly; the Body Center team members agreed to not push forward so strongly before concerns and questions were resolved.

Relationships, which required the most amount of attention, were addressed by scheduling team-building retreats.

Step 6 | Analyze team interactions based on specific type orientations
Eights have big energy and influence even when they are small in number on a team. This team had 10 Eights, more than any other type, and the strength of their influence can be overwhelming to other team members. Although Eights like having this kind of big impact, they realized that it would be best for the team if all the type Eights learned to slow down their responses and be more receptive to other team members' ideas and reactions.

In addition, because there was only one Four in such a large team, this person agreed to speak up more, and other team members agreed to support this.

Team Maps for communication and problem-solving

There are even more ways to use the Enneagram as a team map. One particularly useful way is grouping the nine Enneagram types into three trios: the Optimistic trio (Seven, Nine and Two), the Intensity trio (Four, Six and Eight), and the Competency trio (One, Three and Five). This trio grouping provides insight into how a team communicates and how they go about solving problems.

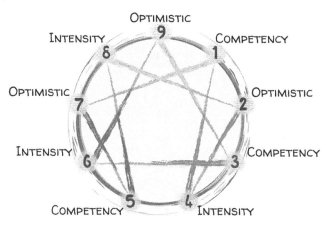

Optimistic trio

Seven, Nine and Two

The three types in the Optimistic trio have a positive overlay on reality so that the world looks better than it actually is. I sometimes say that these three types take a "happy pill" each morning. Sevens take a whole pill, Nines take a half-pill and Twos take a quarter pill.

Sevens are the most optimistic, taking a positive view of just about everything. Nines are moderately positive, perceiving people and events as generally pleasant and congenial. Finally, Twos want and try to see the best in other people – that is, until they don't! The optimism of these three types impacts their communication style and their approach to problem-solving.

Impact on communication style

The three types in the Optimistic trio communicate in an upbeat and positive way. They smile more regularly than the other Enneagram types and tend to be more relationship-oriented. In addition, compared to the other types, the Optimistic trio is more playful and fun-loving. They also like to engage with and talk to other team members more than the types in the other two trios.

Problem-solving approach

Types in the Optimistic trio like to focus on how things can go well rather than how they may go wrong, at least at first. They like different ideas and perspectives and value all team members participating in problem-solving conversations. They will also try to draw out team members who are not saying very much.

Intensity trio

Four, Six and Eight

Types Four, Six and Eight are the most intense of the nine Enneagram types. Their intensity, however, comes from different sources.

The Fours' intensity is emotional, a result of many feelings ruminating and replaying inside them. They have a deep appreciation for intense, authentic interactions. The Sixes' intensity is more mental, the result of their ever-active minds playing and replaying various possible scenarios. The Eights' intensity is more somatic and comes from the body. It is often observed that people can feel the intense presence of Eights, even when Eights are saying absolutely nothing.

Intensity, whether emotional, mental or somatic, is a very strong energy that impacts their communication style and their approach to problem-solving.

Impact on communication style

The three types in the Intensity trio can get quite passionate when they communicate with others. They are also quickly reactive when they like or dislike ideas or a team dynamic. In addition, they like to get to the root or source of the issues and are willing to take the time to do so in-depth.

Problem-solving approach

The types in the Intensity trio like to get it all on the table, even when the topics are delicate and especially when they require a deep discussion. They will also push the team to make this happen and do so in a direct and intense way.

Competency trio

One, Three and Five

The three types in the Competency trio want to both experience themselves as highly competent and want to be treated by others as if they are highly competent. Competency has a different meaning to each of these types.

For Ones, competency means being right, knowing how to organize in the best way, and having the most correct opinion. For Threes, competency means knowing how and being able to move things forward, being able to get great results, and understanding something that they think they should know. For Fives, competency means being capable in terms of their depth and breadth of knowledge and understanding how things fit together.

The competency orientation of Ones, Threes and Fives impacts their communication style and their approach to problem-solving.

Impact on communication

The types in the Competency trio communicate in a clear and concise way, although they may not say exactly what is on their minds or what they feel. They tend to be highly pragmatic and dislike what they consider to be a waste of time. Talking too much or too long is a time-waster. Discussing emotions for too long is, in their view, also a waste of time and uncomfortable to do.

Problem-solving approach

The three types in the Competency trio like a linear, cerebral problem-solving approach to almost everything a team deals with. From their perspective, this is a practical way to deal with issues and allows them to move on and move forward quickly. No frills, no fluff and no wasted time.

How each trio perceives the other two trios

Optimistic trio perceptions of the Intensity trio

Can like the depth of the Intensity trio, but also see the intensity as un-necessary and too serious

Optimistic trio perceptions of the Competency trio

Like the pragmatism of the Competency trio, but can find them too cerebral, linear and not warm enough

Intensity trio perceptions of the Optimistic trio

Enjoy the positivity of the Optimistic trio, but can also see them as not deep enough or avoiding aspects of reality

Intensity trio perceptions of the Competency trio

Like the logic and pragmatism of the Competency trio, but see them as lacking emotionality

Competency trio perceptions of the Optimistic trio

Enjoy the positivity of the Optimistic trio, but want problem-solving to go faster in a more logical way

Competency trio perceptions of the Intensity trio

Like the deeper exploration of issues of the Intensity trio, but want them to be less intense

With all of these ideas in mind, a team can analyze their communication and problem-solving approaches. After that, they can make some choices about what they want to change.

Team map 4 based on the three trios

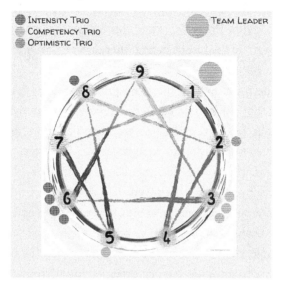

On this high-level executive team, five team members are from the Intensity trio, four are from the Competency trio, and there is a lone team member from the Optimistic trio. An easy way to understand their communication is that it is very intense. About half of the team members express themselves with strength and force and are passionate about what they say. The other half express themselves in more measured and cerebral ways. This has been an issue for the team, creating some challenges for the team leader in facilitating meetings.

The solo Optimistic trio, type Two, says very little during team meetings even though this person is extremely talented and not particularly quiet outside team meetings. In fact, the type Two wishes several things: (1) that the team's communication had less advocacy of position and more inquiry about everyone's reaction, (2) that they allowed more time for the conversations instead of being so fast-paced, and (3) that the team focused more on people's deeper feelings and responses.

In terms of problem-solving, with so many Intensity and Competency types, this team functions primarily on problem-solving using linear thinking. Their focus is on identifying the problem or issue and then figuring out how to fix it. However, they do all this with a great deal of intensity.

By contrast, the lone Optimistic trio team member wants them to explore more possibilities when they think about what to do. In other words, don't start with "define the problem and create a solution." Start with "clarify what we most want in the future, define where are we now, and create a plan for how we can get there."

What can the team do with these insights? Teams are fully capable of deciding what they want to do based on these team map insights, with or without someone facilitating the conversation. The more the team itself decides what they want to do, the more empowered they feel, and the more likely it will be that what they decide will actually happen.

Sometimes simply having a conversation about the team's dynamics changes the way the team functions. At other times, teams will choose to make concrete changes in the way they operate.

As an example, this 10-person executive team would be best served to find the optimal balance between communicating passionately, with five Intensity trio types, and communicating cerebrally, with four team members from the Competency trio. Leaders almost always influence the team dynamics more than any other single team member, so this team was even more weighted toward cerebral communication.

What about the importance of also communicating in a more lighthearted, relationship-oriented way? The lone Optimistic type Two would need to speak up more, and the other team members would need to be more receptive to this way of engaging each other. In other words, would "lightening up" and not being so serious and intense about everything support them as a team? Yes!

What about how this team problem solves? With so many Intensity and Competency trio types, the good news is that they already have a productive problem-solving process. With so many Intensity trio types, they do dig deep into the root causes of challenges facing them. With several Competency trio types, including the team leader, the team also has a practical approach to solving problems.

What's missing is the way in which the Optimistic trio types approach problems – considering alternative ways of addressing and solving issues. Exploring possibilities and thinking out of the box would help them be more innovative. The team might also have more fun working together on these challenges.

There are many other possibilities of using team maps to support a team's understanding of how it functions. For example, because there are three versions of each type called subtypes, team members of each subtype emphasize different areas.

Self-preservation subtypes emphasize trust, resources, safety and structure. Social subtype team members focus on team relationships, cohesion and bonding. One-to-one subtypes emphasize connections between each team member rather than the team as a whole, as well as emotional expression and close relationships. More on the Enneagram subtypes can be found in the Resources at the back of this book.

Maps for solving difficult team challenges

Have you ever been on a team that had a problem for which there seemed to be no possible solution?

That's exactly what I encountered working with a multi-national senior-level team. I had no idea there was an unsolvable problem when they'd asked me to do a day-long Enneagram session to learn the system, their types, and how to apply the insights to their teamwork.

After the first four hours of the program, I was sitting with the team leader during the lunch break and asking some questions about the team. I said, "Your team seems engaged in the program, but they seem to be holding themselves back in a subtle way. Is there something about the team or the program I should know about?"

The team leader said, "Not that I can think of, but maybe you should ask the team."

When they returned from lunch, I asked them the question. This is what they said: "We like the program, but tomorrow we are supposed to create goals for the next six months. We've also been told that within the next three months, there will be a major reorganization in our company. Our team may be entirely disbanded. Our team could be split up and reassigned to leaders of other teams. We don't even know if our leader or any of us will be in our current positions. We're sorry that we're distracted by this. We're good at solving problems, but we have no idea how to solve this one."

Neither did I, but when I do any team program in-person, I always carry a large Enneagram symbol printed on fabric that can be used in a variety of ways. I never know when I might need it. I pulled it out and asked them if they would be willing to try an experiment that just might work. They said yes because they were desperate.

I placed the Enneagram symbol large map on the floor and asked the team leader to stand on type Eight. This was the leader's Enneagram type. In full view of the entire team, I gave these directions and asked the leader to answer these questions out loud, while the team was observing.

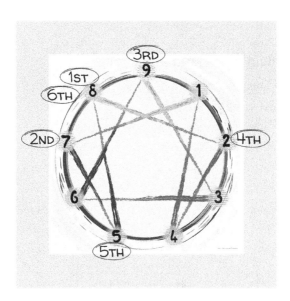

1st Stand on type Eight

Please verbalize the challenge you and your team are facing.
What feelings, thoughts, and concerns do you have about this issue?

2nd Move to type Seven

What insights from type Seven do you have about this issue?
Move back to type Eight.
Please take a breath in silence.

3rd Move to type Nine

What insights from type Nine do you have about this issue?
Move back to type Eight.
Please take a breath in silence.

4th Move to type Two

What insights from type Two do you have about this issue?
Move back to type Eight.
Please take a breath in silence.

5th Move to type Five

What insights from type Five do you have about this issue?

6th Move back to type Eight

Please take a breath in silence.

Please verbalize your thoughts, feeling and insights about this challenge now. What answer do you have to share about your team's dilemma?

To explain the sequence used, we started at type Eight because that was the team leader's Enneagram type.

The next move was to type Seven because it is the number right before the leader's type number (a wing of Eight). This was done because when we identify our own type accurately, we may also have a connection, although a lesser one, to the types on either side of our own type.

Next came a move to type Nine, the number directly after type Eight (also a wing of Eight).

Next was the move to the two different lines that connect to the person's own type. In this case, the move was to type Two, and then the next move was to type Five. *After each move, the person returns to their own type to integrate insights from the other type.*

The team leader, even after only four hours of Enneagram training, arrived at a solution that every single team member understood and agreed would work. Because this happened about six years ago and the solution was highly specific to their context, I can't remember what the resolution was. That's not the point, anyway.

The point is that the Enneagram map, combined with the nine perspectives it contains, produced the amazing insight for this team. Lucky for me and for the team that the team leader was willing to take a risk. Now, they had something they could actually do.

There are many ways to use the Enneagram map to solve challenging team issues. The approach used in this case is just one way to move a team from confusion to clarity to accelerated action.

Do or do not. There is no try.

—YODA

GREAT IDEAS

TEAM MAPS

Great Idea | Buy an Enneagram floor map

If you are intrigued by using the Enneagram as a map, you can buy an Enneagram floor map. When you use it, you'll experience the power of the Enneagram through your whole body. You can purchase lightweight, washable floor maps at TheEnneagramInBusiness.com store.

Great Idea | Experiment with the map

Put the map on the floor, and walk slowly around the circle in a clockwise direction. What do you experience at each type number? You can also stand on your own type number, then follow the arrows in sequence. What do you experience? Keep experimenting with different ways of using the map.

Great Idea | Ask the map a question

If you have an unresolved question, ask the map! Just make sure the question is an open-ended question and not a *yes/no* question. You get better answers this way. You can stand on the map at your Enneagram type, ask the question and get the answer. If you want more information beyond that from your own type, you can use the process just described in this chapter. You can go to any other type number you want, ask the same question and get the answer from that perspective.

Go to Resources for more ideas and details.

TEAM LEADERSHIP

Leaders who think they are leading and have no one
following them are only taking a walk.

—MALAWI PROVERB

"**DO YOU KNOW WHAT LEADERSHIP IS?**" I once asked this question to Warner Burke PhD, author of numerous leadership books and considered to be a leadership authority. "Why are there thousands of leadership books available and in almost every language?"

His answer was straightforward: "Because no one really knows what leadership is!"

At first, I found his answer perplexing, but also insightful. What leadership really is depends on so many factors. What makes a person a great leader involves even more.

I've been working with leaders at every level and in almost every industry for over 40 years. When I ask leaders to describe their leadership style, they typically pause. After the pause, they often have no answer, or they offer a one word or one phrase response. Some say, "I'm a facilitative leader." Others say, "I lead by example." Still others offer, "I lead through vision." While all these answers may be true, each person's leadership style is much more robust and complex than can be captured in a single word or a short phrase.

Why is it so hard to describe their leadership style? Part of the answer is that this is what leaders do daily, so they don't really pause to think about how

[handwritten: each style is good and needed. Believe that your voice needs to be heard / because your perspective matters. Speak up!]

they are leading or why they are doing it. The other part of the answer is perspective. Just as a fish doesn't recognize it is swimming in water, so leaders often don't have a perspective on what seems to be their natural way of leading.

The Enneagram actually provides this perspective because our leadership styles are an outgrowth of our Enneagram types. These nine different leadership styles reflect what leaders of each type think is most important, what they pay the most attention to, and what they tend to ignore. These leadership styles also create our leadership strengths and our areas for development.

One leadership style

A leader's job is to set clear goals and inspire others to achieve the highest quality.

> Strengths: Clarity, pragmatism
> Development areas: Relaxing control, delegation

Two leadership style

A leader's job is to assess the strengths and weaknesses of team members and motivate and facilitate people toward the achievement of organizational goals.

> Strengths: Empathy, motivating others
> Development areas: Setting boundaries, delivering difficult information

Three leadership style

A leader's job is to create an environment that achieves results because people understand the organization's goals and structure.

> Strengths: Getting results, staying focused
> Development areas: Impatience, being afraid to take risks and fail

Four leadership style

A leader's job is to create organizations that give people meaning and purpose so that they are inspired to do excellent work.

> Strengths: Creating deep vision, connecting with others emotionally
> Development areas: Not taking things personally, regulating feelings

Five leadership style

A leader's job is to develop an effective organization through research, deliberation and planning, so that all systems fit together and people are working on a common mission.

Strengths: Objectivity, logical analysis

Development areas: Approachability, emotional connectivity

Six leadership style

A leader's job is to solve organizational problems by developing a creative problem-solving environment in which each person feels that he or she is part of the solution.

Strengths: Problem-solving, perceiving alternative pathways

Development areas: Too little or too much risk-taking, skepticism

Seven leadership style

A leader's job is to get people excited and to create innovative ideas and ventures so that the organization can take advantage of new and important business opportunities.

Strengths: Innovative, enlisting others in the vision

Development areas: Being able to stay focused, adhering to limits

Eight leadership style

A leader's job is to move the organization forward by leading decisively, getting capable and reliable people into the right jobs, and empowering competent people to take action.

Strengths: Taking charge, being assertive

Development areas: Being receptive, over-extending

Nine leadership style

A leader's job is to help achieve the collective mission by creating a clearly structured and harmonious work environment.

Strengths: Creating consensus, listening to multiple perspectives

Development areas: Taking a firm stand, facing conflict directly

Effective team leaders of all Enneagram types need to honor these leadership strengths and work on their development areas.

At the same time, they also need to be able to respond to the team's needs and to adjust their own leadership behavior based on the team's stage of development. This agility may not seem natural to them, but it supports the team's alignment, attunement and acceleration into high performance. The inability to adjust leadership style not only hinders the team's progress, it can actually stall it.

The only way I've ever seen a team make progress through the four stages of team development from *Forming* all the way to *Performing* without an effective and flexible leader is when the team develops ways to bypass the leader. In other words, the leader becomes irrelevant. This is rare and not ideal because leaders play an important role in any team.

That said, there are teams that are specifically organized to be leaderless and self-designing. With these self-organizing teams, the organization usually provides them with more support and resources as a substitute for not having a designated leader. In these teams, natural leaders may emerge who then provide some of the needed leadership functions.

Leaders also play specific roles at each of the four stages of team development. At each stage, the leader needs to be agile and responsive in three different areas: team tasks, team relationships and the leader-team relationship.

STAGE	TASK FOCUS	RELATIONSHIP FOCUS	LEADER–TEAM RELATIONSHIP
Forming	provide clarity and resources	promote inclusion and cohesion	dependency
Storming	allow operational challenges	support constructive expression of conflict	counter-dependency
Norming	make suggestions only if needed	support expression of ideas	interdependence
Performing	provide guidance and resources if needed	acknowledge great work	independence

Forming stage

Rory is a new leader in an extremely well-known company. The organization's view of leadership development is that new leaders should learn to lead by doing, essentially by trial and error. Rory believed there was a better way and hired me as a leadership coach.

With Rory as the leader of a six-person team, helping the team form around task-related issues had been easy. That's because Rory is so technically agile and a creative problem solver. As a new leader, Rory's coaching questions involved the *Forming* stage relationship and process issues: how to create effective relationships with each team member, but also how to generate cohesion and inclusion within the team as a whole. Rory did this masterfully, bringing each relationship challenge from the *Forming* stage to each coaching conversation – for example, how to structure one-to-one conversations and how often to have them, how to give positive and negative feedback to the team and to individual team members in a productive and timely way and more.

No longer leading through trial and error, Rory formed the team through insight and skill. In fact, Rory received the highest rating of all thirty leaders in the business unit. This was based on employee perceptions of their leader.

Task focus: provide clarity and resources
Leaders need to provide the team with clarity about their purpose or charter. For example, what is the organization asking of this team, what are they expected to deliver and by when, what is the team's structure, what are the roles within the team, and what resources are being made available to them? Leaders need to help the team get aligned around these task-related issues.

Relationship focus: promote inclusion and cohesion
Leaders need to make sure all team members feel included, engaged, and feel they have a voice in team discussions. For example, allow time for team members to get to know one another, make sure to not play favorites in any way, and set up constructive guidelines for information sharing and how team members are expected to treat one another. Leaders need to help the team get attuned to one another.

Leader-team relationship: dependency
Leaders at this stage need to recognize that the team, at least at first, will act in a dependent way toward the leader. It is important for leaders to understand that this is natural, but it will and should change as the team makes progress to the next stages. At the beginning of the *Forming* stage, leaders need to be available to the team as needed and address questions they may

have. As the team starts to form effectively, leaders need to gradually encourage the team to be increasingly more involved in direct communication
with one another and to solicit their participation in decision-making.

Enneagram insights

All team leaders need to maintain a balance between focusing on the team's
tasks and on the team's relationships. Some leaders focus more on the task,
some more on relationships and a few maintain an even balance between
the team's tasks and the team's relationships.

Task-focused leaders

Leaders of the following types naturally focus more on tasks than relationships, so they need to remind themselves to pay equal attention to team
relationships: Enneagram types Ones, Threes, Fives, Sevens and Eights.

Relationship-focused leaders

Leaders of the following types naturally focus more on relationships than
tasks, so they need to remind themselves to pay equal attention to team
tasks: Enneagram types Twos, Fours, Sixes and Nines.

Dependency

Dependency issues can be a challenge for many leaders. Some leaders may
like team dependency, but for different reasons. For example, they may as-
sociate or confuse dependency with closeness, team bonding, cooperation or
cohesion. Leaders with this orientation include Twos, Fours, Sixes and Nines.

Twos	Having people dependent on them makes them feel needed and valued.
Fours	Having people dependent on them makes them feel connected to the team.
Sixes	Having people dependent on them makes them feel like the team is their tribe, thus creating a sense of safety.
Nines	Having people dependent on them makes them feel the team is a cohesive and harmonious unit.

Other leaders may dislike dependency, but for different reasons. These
include Fives and Eights.

Fives	Having people dependent on them makes them feel crowded, insufficiently autonomous, and as if too many demands are being placed on them.
Eights	Having people dependent on them makes them feel squeamish, except on teams where they feel fully responsible for and overly protective of everyone.

Some leaders have ambivalence about teams being dependent on them, particularly Ones and Sevens.

Ones	Having people dependent on them makes them uncomfortable because they like everyone to take responsibility for their work and behavior. However, they may also think that dependent teams are ones that they can guide more easily to self-improvement.
Sevens	Having people dependent on them makes them uncomfortable because dependency can feel like an encroachment on their freedom. However, they may also like aspects of dependency, perceiving it as an affirmation of their authority.

If a leader loves you, they make sure you build your house on rock.

—UGANDAN PROVERB

Storming

Corey started a consulting firm from the ground up, building it into a successful and well-respected firm. As a reward for the forty-person team, Corey held an all-company retreat at a beautiful off-site location, complete with delicious food and wonderful sleeping rooms.

During the all-team meeting, one member raised a concern about overworking, with several other team members agreeing. Corey became reactive and defensive about this and the other issues raised. In Corey's view, the retreat was supposed to be a positive experience. Fortunately for the staff and Corey, an outside facilitator who led the retreat called for a break and had an intense conversation with Corey.

The facilitator explained that the team was expressing an important and natural dynamic in the progress of the team: *Storming*. Corey then received on-the-spot coaching about how a leader should best handle the conflict: not take it personally, listen rather than respond, be open to suggestions, and thank team members for their contributions. With this guidance, the retreat helped move the team through the *Storming* stage.

Task focus: allow operational challenges

Leaders need to expect and get comfortable with team members disagreeing with and critiquing ways in which the team operates, including how the leader functions within the team. Even better is when the team leader solicits operational challenges and encourages a constructive conversation about different ways of functioning.

These challenges can be mild, such as raising issues about meeting times, durations and agendas, or they can be about much bigger issues. Examples of bigger issues include a dramatically different way of organizing how the team works, issues with the leader's leadership style, and conflicts between and among team members. Of course, there are numerous topics for *Storming* that are neither mild nor severe. They are all, however, normal.

Relationship focus: support constructive expression of conflict

Leaders who are highly conflict-avoidant or just uncomfortable with conflict have difficulty supporting the team's constructive expression of conflict.

This can be even more of a challenge if the conflict is about the leader. However, if the leader solicits suggestions and concerns, team members get the message that bringing up issues is really OK. Thanking people who do speak up and asking for others' reactions to the same topic helps reinforce speaking up and constructive conversations.

Setting ground rules or guidelines for having this kind of team conversation also helps. Some ground rules might include: let each person finish what they are saying before another person responds, and speak for yourself and not on behalf of others who can speak for themselves.

Leader-team relationship: counter-dependency

Leaders at this stage need to recognize that the team will act less dependent on the leader and more counter-dependent as it moves into and through the *Storming* stage. Counter-dependence means challenging the leader in mild, moderate or more extreme ways. It is important for leaders to understand that this will and should happen as the team makes progress. It is actually a sign of potential forward movement.

The hardest thing for leaders at this stage is to not take these challenges personally. The best thing for leaders to do is to encourage and be receptive to truthful conversations about the team members and their needs.

Enneagram insights

During the *Storming* stage, leaders of all Enneagram types usually experience this stage as the most challenging of the four stages of team development.

One reason for this is that almost no one is truly comfortable with conflict, and leaders are no exception. In general, there is an order to most peoples' discomfort in situations of conflict.

Most uncomfortable when the conflict is directed at them

Uncomfortable, but not as severely, when they are frustrated or upset with someone else

Still uncomfortable, but not as strongly, when there is conflict among others that they are affected by but are not a main participant

How the leader behaves strongly impacts how effectively and quickly team conflict gets identified and resolved. Here are some important tips for team leaders of all Enneagram types.

> Understand that *Storming* is natural and important; without some *Storming*, the team cannot progress.

> Don't take the *Storming* personally, even if the storm is directed at you.

> If the *Storming* is more than the leader feels comfortable dealing with, bring in an outside, neutral facilitator for a team session that involves dealing with the team's issues.

> Remember, what the team may think they are *Storming* about may not be the actual reason for the *Storming*. For example, while the team might think they are *Storming* about not being informed about a decision, which although true, they might be more upset that some team members get this kind of information and others do not. This could be a storm about perceived favoritism rather than about communication only.

> Recognize that an issue the team is *Storming* about doesn't mean that all team members agree that the particular issue is actually a problem. However, the issue still needs to get discussed and resolved.

> It's the team leader's job to create enough psychological safety for the team to constructively engage in the *Storming* conversations and to create enough openness for team members to express themselves.

> Use a coach to help you reflect on how you respond to conflict, disagreements and challenges so you can do so in the most constructive way possible. The key is for leaders to be neither over-reactive to a *Storming* issue – such as getting very angry – or under-reactive, such as withdrawing. Leaders who yell generate fear rather than conversation, and yelling does not simply refer to voice volume. Yelling can be experienced in harsh words, through aggressive body language and more.

The Enneagram can be helpful to leaders of each type as their teams go through the *Storming* stage. Particularly helpful is understanding how leaders from the Competency, Intensity, and Optimistic trios respond.

Leaders whose Enneagram types are from the Competency trio – Ones, Threes and Fives approach *Storming* from a logical and problem-oriented perspective. They tend to want to identify the facts and move to a solution. However, *Storming* also involves emotions. If these are not expressed, any problem-solving solutions may not get implemented.

Leaders whose Enneagram types are from the Intensity trio – Fours, Sixes and Eights – need to be careful to not react quickly or to be highly intense and passionate when they discuss issues. This intensity can feel overwhelming to team members who are not Intensity trio types and can scare them or cause them to not share what they are thinking and feeling.

Leaders whose Enneagram types are from the Optimistic trio – Sevens, Nines and Twos – may come across as overly positive when difficult issues arise. This gives a message to team members that they should not discuss problems that arise for too long or in too much depth. This message, however, does not help the team move through the *Storming* stage.

The roaring lion kills no prey.

—NIGERIAN PROVERB

Norming

As the team leader of a 15-person team, Leigh decided to have a team *Norming* conversation in a way that would be stimulating and productive. Leigh first shared the likely topics for *Norming* that arose from the *Storming* conversation. These would be the initial topics for *Norming*. Topics included how career development conversations would be conducted, a more efficient and effective process for coordinating work, and how ongoing feedback would be given.

After getting confirmation on these three areas, Leigh asked if there were other issues. There were none. Leigh then focused on one topic at a time, divided team members into three groups of five, and asked each group to brainstorm three possible norms for that specific topic. After the small group discussions, each group shared their three ideas. After these small group reports, the whole team decided on the best new norm for that issue.

Leigh then tasked three different small groups of five to do the same thing. Again, the whole team decided on the best option from among the possibilities from the small groups. The process was followed for the third area where new norms were needed: new groups of five, new topic, same process.

This way of creating new norms was not only extremely effective and efficient, team members also felt empowered to make the decisions and got to know one another better in the process.

Task focus: make suggestions only if needed

Leaders have an important function at this stage, and an important part of that role is to hold back your own thoughts and responses, at least initially. This allows team members to become more active and engaged in making suggestions and coming to decisions about new norms and ways of operating. These can be new agreements about the task of the team or the way it is organized.

There are times for leaders to offer suggestions, but the less leaders do, the more the team will do.

Relationship focus: support expression of ideas

Leaders play an important role in encouraging all team members to speak up and express their ideas. To do this, a leader can say at the start of the *Norming* conversation, "For every issue we discuss, let's hear from everyone before deciding." This statement is actually a suggested norm, so it can be followed by, "Is this OK with everyone?"

At different times in the conversation, the leader can say, "Does everyone agree with this idea?" or "Let's hear from everyone before deciding." In this last statement, there is a subtle message. The word "Let's" means "Let us all hear from everyone" and thus focuses on the team.

This is a very different message than "I want to hear from everyone before I decide." This last statement conveys the message that the leader wants to hear from everyone and then the leader will decide what to do about the issue being discussed. This kind of leader-directed message does not help accelerate the team forward. Instead, it reinforces dependency on the leader and can take the team back to the *Forming* stage. It can also create a counter-dependent reaction within the team where team members push back on the leader. This can take the team back to the *Storming* stage.

Leader-team relationship: interdependence

Leaders at this stage need to share responsibility with the team so that the relationship between the leader and the team is one of mutual interdependence. Leaders definitely have a role to play. Stepping back from the team entirely does not support the team's development. Neither does being too active too early, too often or offering too much direction.

In addition, some of the new norms that need to be created may have to do with the leader. For example, the team may think that the leader is too involved in team decisions or not involved enough. The leader needs to be open to the discussion and seek to understand what is being said rather than to be reactive.

Enneagram insights
Responses to *Norming* challenges and growth areas

During the *Norming* stage, leaders of all Enneagram types experience challenges. Some of these challenges include: how much to say or not say, how much to do or not do, and how to have their points of view included in the conversation without getting in the way of the team's progress toward interdependence with the leader. In addition, many leaders at this stage also need to give up some degree of control of the team. Here are the *Norming* stage challenges and growth areas for leaders of each Enneagram type.

Enneagram One typical Norming responses

Challenges: Liking to assert your opinions; giving ideas for how to improve things; making sure the way the team operates is under control

Growth: Listening more; holding back suggestions about how to operate unless the team truly needs your ideas; relaxing your need to control smaller items

Enneagram Two typical Norming responses

Challenges: Actively wanting to help the team make progress; over-facilitating team conversations

Growth: Reminding yourself that the more the team does for itself, the more you are helping them grow; taking pleasure in their increasing independence

Enneagram Three typical Norming responses

Challenges: Being impatient with the length of the *Norming* process; offering suggestions for norms too early to get fast results

Growth: Reminding yourself that an effective *Norming* process is as important as the final new norms; increasing your patience

Enneagram Four typical Norming responses

Challenges: Speaking too early about what you want; reacting too quickly to what others suggest

Growth: Observing and enjoying the process; being careful about sharing or showing non-verbally what you like or dislike

Enneagram Five typical Norming responses

Challenges: Wanting team conversations to be much shorter; discomfort when team members express feelings

Growth: Observing the dynamics of the process as a way to learn about the team; encouraging the sharing of feelings

Enneagram Six typical Norming responses

Challenges: Being less reactive to thoughts and feelings expressed; feeling anxious as the team is deliberating

Growth: Staying calm and centered; allowing team conversations to proceed fluidly and emergently

Enneagram Seven typical Norming responses

Challenges: Being unfocused through longer team discussions; sharing too many ideas

Growth: Listening rather than speaking; allowing the team to establish norms even if you think they might limit you

Enneagram Eight typical Norming responses

Challenge: Needing to exert control over the conversation; listening to ideas only from those you respect

Growth: Staying receptive to new ideas; not taking suggestions as an authority challenge

Enneagram Nine typical Norming responses

Challenge: Over-facilitating the team; not sharing own thoughts

Growth: Staying present even if tensions arise; not appearing to agree with an idea through head-nodding if you don't actually agree

Great acts are made up of small deeds.

—LAO TZU

Performing

Celebration! How do leaders know what to do and how to do it? Robin solved this dilemma by creating a small, voluntary team selected from within the twenty-person team. Their task was to be in charge of celebrations.

Robin empowered them to make all decisions, gave them a budget based on what they requested, and served as a resource as needed. Everyone on the celebration team loved it, participated in whatever way requested, and

Robin did very little except enjoy how well this worked and how positively the whole team responded to whatever was planned.

Task focus: provide guidance and resources if needed

Leaders of teams at the *Performing* stage still play an important function for the team. They can be guides on the side, allowing team members to come to them when needed. At the same time, high-performing teams still need resources to do their work. These resources are often in areas only the leader can authorize or provide.

In addition, teams at the *Performing* stage still run into organizational obstacles with other parts of the organization. Here the team leader can advise the team itself on how to overcome these or may need to get actively involved. Team leaders can still raise issues for the team but should help the team solve most of these themselves rather than immediately stepping into an active role. The idea is to promote their capability, resilience and independence.

Relationship focus: acknowledge great work

Team leaders at *Performing* stages serve the team best by being coaches and cheerleaders. At this stage, the saying "Less is more" applies, yet teams always need positive reinforcement and acknowledgment for specific successes – for example, meeting deadlines on time or delivering below budget. Perhaps the team was dealing with a difficult issue that they solved themselves. This is a time to celebrate.

Learn the many ways to celebrate and find out what your specific team enjoys by way of celebration. Some teams like time off, while others appreciate gift certificates. Many times, a thoughtful email or thank-you card makes a big difference.

Celebrations can and should be done at the team level with all team members, but individual celebrations, whether done individually or acknowledged in the team, are also appreciated. Consider birthdays, new children or grandchildren, the completion of a university degree or an important training program. As a leader, show you care and get creative.

Please remember that some people dislike any form of public acknowledgment, others appreciate it and some people crave it. Be sensitive to different needs. All you have to do is ask people what they like and don't like!

Leader-team relationship: independence

Leaders at this stage need to recognize that the team has achieved the *Performing* stage because of the team's performance, but also because of your guidance, support and flexibility. As a leader, you've adjusted your team leadership style to meet the needs of the team. You didn't drive and control the team all the way.

In fact, the team's success is because you encouraged their independence. And they will still need you in some ways. Exactly how they need you depends on the complexity of their work and the issues that arise outside the team – for example, a company reorganization, a change in customer base, a reduction of resources, the addition of new team responsibilities. Be open, be available, and give them the space and support they need to continue their high performance.

Servant Leadership

Team leaders are ideally stewards of their teams. The concept of stewardship comes from the work of Servant Leadership. This means that the leader is there to serve the team and the organization. In other words, the team does not serve the leader and the leader is not self-serving.

A self-serving leader seeks to gain money, status, prestige, power or control.

A servant leader is more conscious, has more integrity and more humility.

What does a servant leader do? Here are the gifts and perspectives on servant leadership from the nine Enneagram types. Please take these servant leader descriptions as archetypes rather than a gift that only applies to one Enneagram type. Leaders of all Enneagram types can embrace these nine perspectives as they aspire to be stewards of their teams.

Enneagram One perspective
Growing others

Team leaders who act as stewards believe that people have an intrinsic value beyond their tangible contributions as workers and are deeply committed to the growth and improvement of every individual and team.

STEWARDSHIP

GROWING OTHERS
LISTENING
PERSUASION
EMPATHY
FORESIGHT
RESPONSIBILITY
BIG PICTURE
FULL AWARENESS
BUILDING COMMUNITY

Enneagram Two perspective
Listening

Team leaders who act as stewards have a deep commitment and ability to listen intently to others and to also sense the "will" of the team.

Enneagram Three perspective
Persuasion

Team leaders who act as stewards use persuasion rather than continuously using positional authority to make things happen. They build respect, influence and consensus because the overuse of positional authority erodes respect for the leader. Stewards use positional authority sparingly and only when absolutely required.

Enneagram Four perspective
Empathy

Team leaders who act as stewards understand and empathize with other people, but also accept and acknowledge them as individuals even if they do not agree with them.

Enneagram Five perspective
Foresight

Team leaders who act as stewards possess foresight, which enables them to understand the lessons from the past, the realities of the present, and the likely consequences of a decision or action. This requires both intuition and the ability to trust oneself.

Enneagram Six perspective
Responsibility

Team leaders who act as stewards assume a commitment to serving the needs of others, including those who their organization or unit serves. The attitude is not one of "owning the team or organization;" it is one of having the honor of "holding the team and organization in trust" for others.

Enneagram Seven perspective
Big picture

Team leaders who act as stewards perceive the whole as well as the parts; they see the forest, trees, branches, leaves and roots. They also know what they need to take action on and when some things simply resolve themselves.

Enneagram Eight perspective
Full awareness

Team leaders who act as stewards have self-awareness, awareness of others, and awareness of what is occurring in the environment. They see reality as it is, not a distorted version.

Enneagram Nine perspective
Building community

Team leaders who act as stewards stand at the helm of their team, guiding it in times of certainty and uncertainty. This guidance is always with a keen sense of having a positive impact on the various affected communities.

When the best leader's work is done, the people say,
'We did it ourselves.'

—LAO TZU

GREAT IDEAS

TEAM LEADERSHIP

Great Idea | Answer this important question
"Why would someone want to be led by you?" Write down as many answers to this question as you can. To be a leader, people should want to be led by you, so you need to know the answer to this question.

Great Idea | Get feedback on your team leadership style
It can be challenging for leaders to ask for feedback, plus there's always the issue of whether or not people feel safe enough and sufficiently skilled to give feedback effectively. As a leader, it is important to ask for specific rather than general feedback. What do you really want to know, and who do you want answers from? You can ask individuals directly, you can use a survey in which respondents remain anonymous, or you can use a consultant to do interviews.

Great Idea | Learn more about your leadership style
Our overall leadership styles grow directly out of our Enneagram types. You can learn more about your leadership style from the book "What Type of Leader Are You?" by Ginger Lapid-Bogda. From this book, you'll also gain insights into your type-based strengths and development areas in eight different leadership competency areas.

CHAPTER 12

MORE ABOUT TEAMS

When the threads unite, they can tie the lion.

~AFRICAN PROVERB

OF COURSE, THERE'S MORE TO TEAMS than becoming increasingly aligned, attuned and accelerating. There's also more to teams than the transformation from a "possible team" to an "actual team" to a "high-performing" one. And there's more than effectively navigating from *Forming*, through *Storming*, then *Norming* and, ultimately, *Performing*.

What about team-based rewards?

I've had countless conversations over the years, even debates, with colleagues about whether a team must also have team-based rewards to be considered a team. Some colleagues have even insisted that team-based rewards must be added to common goals and interdependence as the third criteria for what it means to be a team.

My view is that team rewards really matter in order to reinforce teaming and team-enhancing behavior. In other words, team rewards need to be linked directly to what is being asked of the team.

Generally, rewards linked to specific team behaviors reinforce these behaviors. Team rewards not linked to specific behaviors are nice to have but have limited impact on team performance. In addition, it is important to also have individually-based rewards, also linked to specific desired behavior. Rewarding team-based behavior only can be a de-motivator for some team members.

In sum, I think team rewards greatly enhance teaming but are not at the same level as goals and interdependence as defining criteria.

What's the role of team communication and coordination?

All teams need ways of effectively communicating with one another and coordinating their work. Exactly how best to do this varies from team to team. In general, communication and coordination needs are related to team interdependence. The more interdependent a team needs to be, the greater the need for effective communication and coordination.

Is there more to team leadership?

There's even more to team leadership than leaders being agile and re-sponsive to their teams at the four stages of team development. There's more to leadership than being servant leaders rather than self-serving ones.

Leaders also serve as team architects who are responsible for creating or co-creating: team culture, team vision, strategy, structure, roles, processes, the ability to attract and retain team talent, and a commitment to high-quality products and services.

Great and terrible leaders for any team

Great team leaders also need to have good character and share these qual-ities, creating trust and safety within the team and inspiring the team and its members to do their best.

GREAT TEAM LEADERS

available · praises · truthful · empathic · patient · realistic
integrity · listens well · non-discriminatory · encourages
cares about employees · trustworthy · supports careers
respectful · forthcoming · humble · open-minded · inclusive
self-managing · considers others · takes responsibility

Terrible team leaders share these qualities, creating fear and distrust within the team and demotivating the team and its members on an everyday basis.

TERRIBLE TEAM LEADERS

yells · not available · interrupts · constantly criticizes
undermines · creates fear · betrays trust · condescends
micromanages · discriminatory · gossips · disrespectful · lies
breaks promises · takes revenge · shows favoritism
intimidates · blocks careers · doesn't listen · humiliates

You can choose. Be a great team leader!

A candle loses nothing by lighting another candle.

—ITALIAN PROVERB

GREAT IDEAS

MORE ABOUT TEAMS

Great Idea | Select your rewards carefully

People like rewards, but they especially like rewards that are meaningful to them. They also want to know what they need to do to achieve them. Find out what rewards matter to your team and link these rewards to specific team behaviors and milestones. Sometimes surprise rewards are fun and motivating, but be aware that what you think is a reward might not be a reward to different team members.

Great Idea | Improve team communication and coordination

Here's a simple and non-pressuring way for a team to discuss and make improvements in how they communicate and coordinate. Start with this. Ask each team member to share the one thing they like the most about the team. Make sure everyone says something, and repetitions are fine. Then ask this question. If you had a magic wand and could change one thing about how the team communicates and coordinates work, what would that be? Make sure each team member contributes. Finally, take the magic wand list and resolve the issues that seem most important to the team.

Great Idea | Use the list of great and terrible leaders

Look over the list of qualities that make a leader great or terrible. From the list of great leader qualities, select the attributes you want to do more of, and make it your intention to pay attention to doing these. Review the list for terrible leaders. If you do any of these things, stop doing them. If stopping is a challenge for you, use the services of a coach – preferably an Enneagram-savvy coach – to help you understand and change these behaviors.

CHAPTER 13

WHAT'S NEXT?

The first step toward greatness is to be honest.

—TRADITIONAL PROVERB

REMEMBER JORDAN AND BLAIRE who couldn't stand being in the same room at the same time with each other? Like most of us, they discovered through the Enneagram that they were both the problem and the solution.

That awareness can pay huge dividends in the workplace environment.

When team members are more "aware," they are more open to problem-solving and collaboration. That, in and of itself, can be a huge shift in the dynamics of the team. The Enneagram also has a magnifier effect. You start it in one application area, such as your team, and it spreads throughout the organization because of its positive impact.

So what's next now that you know much more about teams and have learned how the Enneagram builds trust, decreases stress and increases productivity?

First, it's totally possible to create a cohesive and high-energy group where everyone feels respected and treated well. And even if you are leading a group that really isn't a team, you will know how to spend your time and resources most effectively because of your own awareness of the interplay between yourself and others.

By contrast, if you lead a team that functions like a group but really should be a team, you can help them become an "actual team" by helping them clarify their common team goals and optimal levels of interdependence.

The Enneagram is an invaluable way to help all team members examine how they define goals, clarify what kind of interdependence they prefer and why, and become more flexible, all in service of the team.

Now perhaps you're a leader who, with all good intentions, wants to use the Enneagram, but needs to resolve the underlying team and leadership issues first. *Remember, lack of psychological safety and team distrust are symptoms of issues; they are not the underlying cause.* When underlying issues need to be addressed, it's often useful to bring in an outside consultant who knows the Enneagram to work with you and your team. The objectivity of the outsider can bring "fresh eyes" to the team and help address deeper issues.

And if you're a team leader now, you may have multiple teams you're responsible for in the future. Just think of how much better you will be at helping your teams align, attune and accelerate into high performance!

But even if you're not the team leader, you can still help your team become more high-performing. You may be a team member today, but tomorrow you might be a team leader.

Here's what you can do.

Start with you. Learn the Enneagram for yourself so you understand how you can engage even more productively on your team.
Choose to shift your type-based behavior, depending on the stage of your team; *even one person shifting behavior can positively influence the entire team!*
Have a meaningful conversation with your team leader and suggest using the Enneagram with your team.
Make a suggestion to the whole team about something that would benefit their growth.
Suggest clarifying team goals and promote inclusion if the team has *Forming* stage issues.
Encourage people to bring up and listen to differing ideas if the team has *Storming* stage challenges.
Suggest possible new norms and ask for responses from other team members if the team is at the *Norming* stage.
Look for ways to offer support to over-worked or stressed team members if the team is at the *Performing* stage.

The Enneagram is an incredible asset to use in the workplace. In addition to transforming teams by building trust, decreasing stress and improving productivity, the Enneagram can also:

Develop conscious and highly-skilled leaders
Reduce miscommunication at all levels in the organization
Encourage innovation, creativity, and productive risk-taking
Help retain talented employees
Change organizational culture to be more collaborative
Improve customer relationships
Increase organizational sustainability

When you integrate the Enneagram into your teams, you'll end up spending less time and money dealing with conflict, you'll reduce your frustration with others, and you'll feel far more satisfied and capable at work than you ever thought possible.

And that's why the Enneagram's impact goes way beyond the workplace – it's dynamic, illuminating and helps people build better relationships wherever they are. People who learn the Enneagram at work bring the Enneagram home to their friends, partners, children and even extended families. It makes a huge difference in all your relationships!

The best way to create transformation in your team is to model transformation in yourself. The more you learn about yourself, the more you are able to respond in ways that can build trust and enable others to want to learn more.

It always comes down to our commitment to our own development. That's why the Enneagram is so powerful individually and particularly powerful in teams. When we are able to bring our best and highest selves, we are often able to bring out the best and highest in others we work with.

The best knowledge is to know yourself.

—WELSH PROVERB

GREAT IDEAS

WHAT'S NEXT?

Great Idea | Get more team-Enneagram resources

Just email us, and we'll send you these three items, all in pdf and color: the four questions to identify each type from Chapter 3 The Enneagram; the Psychological Safety Assessment from Chapter 4; and a special Q&A document about teams and the Enneagram. You have our full permission to print and use these items as long as you keep our © on the documents. Email: info@theenneagraminbusiness.com

Great Idea | Find the highest-quality coaches, trainers, consultants and training tools

The Enneagram in Business provides coaching, training, and consulting services that fully integrate the Enneagram in a wide variety of organizational applications. We also have an excellent Enneagram in Business Network of highest quality professionals across the globe.

If you want coaching, training and consulting services, contact us.
Email: info@theenneagraminbusiness.com

If you want 28 full-color, hard copy training tools, go to our store.
Website: TheEnneagramInBusiness.com

Great Idea | Share the Enneagram with those you care about

The Enneagram spreads in so many ways, but especially through word-of-mouth. So if you like it for yourself, tell others about it. The Enneagram can be used beyond organizational use, such as deep personal development, becoming a better parent, gaining more spiritual access, teaching more effectively, dealing with trauma and addictions and more.

Go to Resources for more ideas and details.

ACKNOWLEDGMENTS

People acknowledgments

Most important has been Gwen Baker-Yuill, in more areas than I can mention: illustrations, honest and useful feedback, copy editing and more. Next, my son, Russell (Tres) Bogda for his feedback and edits. The book layout design is the beautiful work of Jeanna Wiggins, while credit for the book cover goes to the talented David Fassett. There is also Karen Anderson, who is super smart about everything related to books, who offered crucial ideas at just the right time.

In addition, this book would not exist without my many clients over the years who allowed me to work with their teams and gain so much experience. Without them, there would also be no stories for this book. All the book's stories and examples are real, but names have been changed for a number of reasons: client confidentiality, my intention to be gender-neutral, but also race, age and, in every other way, neutral. Why? Because the stories stand as excellent examples of team and leader behavior no matter the gender, race, age or geography.

I want to also acknowledge the people for whom I wrote this book. I wrote it for team leaders who want to accelerate their teams, team members who want to help their teams excel, and serious and competent coaches, trainers and consultants who want to use the Enneagram with teams in the best of ways. Special thanks to Chloé Keric-Eli, Peter O'Hanrahan, Jennifer Joss, Mary Maddock and Sharon Ball who listened as I used them as sounding boards for many of my ideas.

Next, thanks to some broad shoulders on which I stand. First is NTL (National Training Labs), where I have been a member since the early 1990s. This is the place where almost all major behavioral science models were created. And if they were not created through NTL, the creators were NTL members. I've taught many programs for NTL over the years, and my exposure to models and knowledge leaders has been foundational to my conceptual understanding and my ability to put models into practice. I especially want to thank four people who were my teaching partners and left important legacies: Phil Hanson, Uma Umapathy and Lindy Sata from NTL (National Training Labs) and Joseph Luft (the Jo part of the Johari Window), who was my teaching partner at UCLA. There's also Beverly Kaye, my dear friend, who showed me almost everything I know about creating delicious training materials and the importance of having fun while you work.

Finally, I am also indebted to some of the greatest contemporary Enneagram teachers: Helen Palmer, Don Riso and Claudio Naranjo. I am in gratitude to have been so fundamentally influenced by these three super-smart and beautifully committed world-class thinkers and teachers. Thank you all!

Concept acknowledgments

I believe it is essential to acknowledge where the concepts we use originated and to give credit where credit is due. Here are the original sources for the concepts used in this book.

Alignment and attunement

This concept (without my addition of acceleration) is generally attributed to a consulting firm called Innovation Associates and to consultant Roger Harrison, in particular, who was affiliated with the firm.

Team goals and interdependence

The importance of common team goals and collective responsibility (interdependence) for achieving them is most clearly articulated in *The Wisdom of Teams* by Jon Katzenbach and Douglas Smith.

Stages of Team Development Model

The four stages of team development are the original work of Bruce Tuckman, who later added a fifth stage, *Adjourning*.

Pinch-Crunch Conflict Model

The Pinch-Crunch Model is the original work of Jack Sherwood and John Glidewell.

Team roles

Team roles, originally called task and maintenance roles, first appeared in the work of K. Benne and P. Sheets.

Servant leadership

Servant leadership is based on the work of Robert Greenleaf.

TEAM TRANSFORMATIONS

Resources

	GROUPS, PLUS TEAM GOALS AND INTERDEPENDENCE ACTIVITIES
DESCRIPTION	Working with groups, teams, team goals, and interdependence
TIME	Varies depending on group size
MATERIALS	None
DIRECTIONS	**What to do with a group that is not a team** Celebrations work really well, for holidays, birthdays and sometimes just as surprises. Handwritten thank-you notes and good-quality chocolate candy are always winners. Maybe there is a topic they'd like to learn more about. Get creative because thoughtfulness goes a long way. **How to identify common team goals** First, identify the team's purpose; what is this team being asked to accomplish? Identifying the team's purpose is often the responsibility of the team leader, but some team leaders like to involve the team because it creates a shared understanding and commitment. Self-designing teams, where there is no formal leader, develop their own team purpose. Next, identify one to five possible common goals that allow the team to achieve its purpose. A goal is a simple statement about a concrete objective that is measurable and has a realistic date by which that goal will be achieved. Teams with more than five goals can feel overwhelmed, so keep it simple. Brainstorm possible goals, where everyone contributes ideas without any judgment. Then select from among the possibilities in terms of which goals most contribute to the team's purpose. This process is engaging and dynamic. **How to determine optimal level of team interdependence** After the team's goals are identified, take each team goal, one at a time. For each goal, identify precisely who is dependent on who to accomplish that goal. Think of this as a relay race with team members as multiple runners, each having a distinct baton. As the "hand-off" is identified, also be very specific about what the "hand-off" concretely involves. Do this until all the "hand-offs" have been identified for each goal. Identify the "hand-offs" both verbally and visually. When you are in person, have all team members stand in a circle, each with a long pencil. Start with one person, who has a rolled-up ball of string so that the ball of string is easy to throw. Have that person identify another team member on whom they have a dependency and say that person's name along with the nature of the dependency. The first person then throws the ball of string to that person. The second person throws the ball of string to a third person, again saying the new person's name and exact "hand-off." A web of interdependencies is created like a spider's web. Just make sure the ball of string throws well and unravels as you throw. If you are remote, follow the above activity guidelines, but use a whiteboard. Do a team assessment. Are the interdependencies the optimal ones needed to achieve the goals or are there (1) too many, (2) too few, or (3) not the right ones? Make agreements as a team to make changes in the "hand-offs" in order to maximize optimal interdependence. In addition, are there some team members who have a great number of strings or lines coming in their direction? These team members are called "hubs." Are these people in key roles? Are they overloaded? Make adjustments as needed.

ICE BREAKER ACTIVITIES

DESCRIPTION	Very short questions to use at the start of programs that help participants feel more at ease with one another
TIME	Depends on group size and whether these questions are answered in the large group, in smaller break-out groups, or even in chat (if virtual)
MATERIALS	None, except the chosen question on PowerPoint if desired
DIRECTIONS	**Sample questions to use with participants who don't know the Enneagram** What is your best stress reliever? How does it work? What is something you think has no value? Why? Who is your favorite hero (living or dead)? Why? What is your favorite useless fact? What makes this useless? What contest would you most like to win? Why? Where would you most like to go on a vacation? Why? How did you get your name? **Sample questions to use with participants who already know the Enneagram** What is your best stress reliever? How does it work? How is your choice type related? What is something you think has no value? Why? How is this type related? Who is your favorite hero (living or dead)? Why? How is this type related? What is your favorite useless fact? What makes this useless? How is this type related? What contest would you most like to win? Why? How is this type related? Where would you most like to go on a vacation? Why? How is your choice type related? Ask only one question or it will take too long. Give participants a specific amount of time to share their responses if this is done in a large group. If done in smaller groups, have each group share only one response from their small group conversation when they return to the larger group.

WARM-UP ACTIVITIES

DESCRIPTION	Short activities, slightly longer than ice breakers, used at the start of a training session that help people engage in the program, become involved in initial self-reflection, and connect with the program topic
TIME	Depends on group size and whether these are answered in the large group, in smaller break-out groups, or even in chat (if virtual)
MATERIALS	None, except the question on PowerPoint if desired
DIRECTIONS	**Sample questions to use with participants who don't know the Enneagram as well as those who do** Think of three words that you think describe you well. What are they? Reflect on positive feedback you've received that really surprised you. What was it? Where is your favorite place to relax? Imagine yourself there now and describe what it's like. **Sample questions to use with participants who already know the Enneagram** What is the biggest question you have about your type? What have you discovered about yourself from knowing the Enneagram that you didn't realize before? What is one way your type has been a great asset?
HINTS	Use only one warm-up activity per session. Make the activity take no longer than 30 minutes. Set a time limit per answer if the activity asks for responses. If the activity includes verbal responses from participants, call on each person yourself, or use the "popcorn" method where people speak when they want to speak in a more spontaneous way. Call on one person, then let them select another person who has not yet spoken. If you have a larger group size and you want to hear responses, for in-person programs, break them into small groups of 3-5 people. For virtual programs, use virtual breakout rooms and ask a few people to share their responses when the large group comes back together. Alternatively, use the "chat" function and ask people to write in their answers.

TYPE GROUP DISCUSSION QUESTIONS	
DESCRIPTION	A great way for participants to engage with each other, the material, and to generate Enneagram-based insights
TIME	45 minutes, including reports outs to larger group
MATERIALS	None, except the question(s) for the type groups on PowerPoint
DIRECTIONS	Start with the same compelling question for each type group to answer; choose only one or two questions and have each type group answer the same question(s). If you give them too many questions to discuss, it distracts from the depth of the conversation. Divide participants into groups according to their Enneagram types. Ask them to discuss the question you have chosen. **Sample questions** What do we have in common, and how are we different? Why do we think we're this type, and what is one way we most often get misunderstood? What is our type's greatest gift, and what is our most important development area? What is your ideal work environment, and what work environment is especially difficult for you? If you could give advice to a 12-year-old version of yourself, what would that be? What do you like about teams, and what drives you crazy about them?
HINTS	Type groups will be of different sizes, but all type group conversations should last about 12-15 minutes. If a type group is especially large – over 12 people – divide them into two groups. Have each type group do a one-minute report out to the whole group with one simple question that can be answered in the given time. Reports that go too long are under-stimulating. For reporting out, start with one type and go sequentially through the types. If you start with type One, then go to type Two. If you start at type Four, go next to type Five. Participants will remember the information better if you go in sequence.

TEAM BUILDING ENNEAGRAM SCAVENGER HUNT ACTIVITY

DESCRIPTION	A fun, interactive and high-engagement activity that relates to the Enneagram
TIME	1 hour or more, depending on number of teams
MATERIALS	List of nine items for the scavenger hunt
DIRECTIONS	Divide participants into equal size teams, with each team given a list of nine items to find, with each item representing a specific positive quality of each type. These are then shared with the large group and prizes are awarded (first team finished, most original, or everyone gets a prize). Give them the following directions verbally and provide each team with a list of items to be found. This list can be sent to them electronically if done virtually or handed out as a hard copy for in-person programs. Do not distribute this list in advance of the activity. Find and bring back nine different objects, each object reflecting one of the nine items below: 1. The high-quality orientation of Ones 2. The generosity of Twos 3. The success orientation of Threes 4. The rich internal life of Fours 5. The systematic objectivity of Fives 6. The creative problem-solving ability of Sixes 7. The out-of-the-box thinking of Sevens 8. The deep power of Eights 9. The ability to embrace all perspectives of Nines Return when you have all items with you, making sure you have a clear rationale for selecting each item that can be briefly explained. In addition, have each object with you and select one person to speak on behalf of your team. Tell the teams that when they are finished, return to the main room. Once all teams have returned, have each team explain their items – in order from type One through type Nine – and the rationale for selecting each item. After all teams have reported, give all teams a "prize" for their good work. Award prizes.
HINTS	Multiple teams can do this activity at the same time, divided into equal size teams; team size can be from 4-person teams to 8-person teams. If you have two teams, the total time is approximately 65 minutes. For every additional team, add approximately 10 more minutes to the total time (for team presentations).

TEAM BUILDING ENNEAGRAM BINGO ACTIVITY

DESCRIPTION	A dynamic activity for participants to get to know each other better, "Basic" for those new to the Enneagram or "Bingo Plus" for those with some Enneagram knowledge
TIME	45 minutes, depending on the number of teams
MATERIALS	One bingo card for each participant

DIRECTIONS	Form as many teams as you like but arrange people in same size teams, between six minimum and twelve maximum per team. If the teams are too small, the activity won't work well. Here is the information to give to participants.
	
	"This is like the traditional game of Bingo except you are playing it as a team instead of as individuals. Also, your goal is to fill the whole card, not just a line across. Each of you has a Bingo card, plus we ask that you also have a pen or pencil. When you get into your team breakout groups, find out who on your team can answer each question on your card. Here are the rules:
	
	The object of the game is to get to know each other better and to, if possible, have a team member's name in each box, indicating that this person can answer the question in the box. You'll also need to write down that person's answer.
	    1. Select one team member to keep the Bingo card for the team and write down the names and answers.
	    2. Make the person whose name is written in the box answer the question or statement and tell the team their answer.
	    3. Ideally, each team member's name must be in at least one of the boxes. Sometimes this is not possible, but try!
	    4. When and if you have all boxes filled in, notify the trainers, and come back to the main room.
	    5. Once a team believes their card is complete and has notified the trainers, all teams must stop working on their cards and return to the main room."
	
	The first team to fill every box on the card is the winner. If more than one team completes their card, the team that completed their card first will go first. The trainer asks for the answer from the first team for each box on their card in order to confirm they are a winner. If the first team is not able to answer all questions accurately, the game changes to the following:
	
	The second team with the fewest blank boxes on their Bingo card gets to ask any other participant or trainer (but not a member of the first team) if that person can answer their remaining blank questions and what the answer is. If this person can answer the question, that team writes that person's name and answer in the box and continues until their card is filled. You can give prizes to the winning team or to all teams.

Bingo Basic
Write down the answer in the box

Can name three positive things about self	Has an unusual hobby or interest	Has one very strong principle of value	Can describe their life motto
Knows their life purpose	Has or has had a pet with a human name		Writes or reads poetry
Knows how to give effective constructive feedback	Can name a special 'genius' they have	Loves to read books and can explain why	Is a really good cook
Pursues self-development regularly	Plays a sport well	Is interested in politics	Recently picked up a new hobby

Bingo Plus
Write down the answer in the box

Knows what the word Enneagram means	Can name three characteristics of type One	Can name the three Centers of Intelligence	Has used the Enneagram to resolve conflict
Practices one development activity for their type	Has increased compassion from knowing the Enneagram	Can name one strength of their own type	Can name a metaphor for their type
Can name three characteristics of type Seven		Can name a development activity for type Three	Knows what self-observation means
Has increased self-awareness using the Enneagram	Can name three characteristics of type Eight	Has increased self-acceptance using the Enneagram	Can name three characteristics of type Two

ENNEAGRAM APPLICATION ACTIVITIES	
DESCRIPTION	Real-world applications with a simple design and based on a useful concept; type groups are people of the same type; mixed groups refer to mixing up the types within a group.
TIME	From 15-45 minutes, depending on report-out length
MATERIALS	Materials as needed for a chosen application
DIRECTIONS	**Motivation** *Concept* Motivation and demotivation relate directly to type. *Type groups* Type groups discuss what motivates them, what demotivates them, and what they and/or their managers can do to increase their motivation. *Mixed groups* Give mixed groups a task. An example would be creating a motivational celebration, one that they believe would appeal to the motivational structure of all nine types, but give them a limited amount of time, such as 15 minutes. **Sales** *Concept* People make purchasing decisions based on what they want in both goods and services, and these are related to type. *Type groups* Type groups discuss what they like in terms of goods and services and what they dislike. *Mixed groups* Give mixed groups a sales challenge, for example, how to sell a product to a new client who knows nothing about the product. Give them 15 minutes to choose their approach. Then ask them to rate how satisfied they are with their solution, how well they worked as a group, and how each person's ideas reflected their Enneagram types. **Stress** Concept Enneagram types each have their own stressors and best paths to de-stress. *Type groups* Type groups discuss what stresses them out, how they react to stress and what helps them de-stress. *Mixed groups* Give groups a stressful activity such as a very short, time-limited task where a group has to write down as many stressors that they all have in common. The task should be something that would take 15 minutes to do well, but only give them 5 minutes. Instead of a report to the whole group, ask each group to discuss what stressed them about the activity, how they reacted when stressed, and how their answers reflect their Enneagram types.
HINTS	After type-group discussions, do reports to larger group so everyone is better informed about the differences between the types. Start reports with one type and go sequentially. If a type group is missing, that's OK. You can just not cover that type or give a brief summary if you know it.

THE 27 ENNEAGRAM SUBTYPES

In the chapter on team maps, there's a mention of team mapping based on Enneagram subtypes. To do subtype mapping, the team needs to go beyond their types; team members also need to know their specific subtypes. The term subtype refers to the three sub-versions of each Enneagram type, thus the name subtype. For each Enneagram type, there are three possible subtypes: self-preservation, social and one-to-one. The one-to-one subtype of each type is also called the intimacy or sexual subtype.

Your subtype indicates what areas you pay a great deal of attention to and what areas are less of a concern. It's important to remember that paying attention to something does not mean you like something. It can also mean you avoid something entirely or are ambivalent about it. In other words, you both like it and don't like it, yet it's always on your radar. Here's what the three different subtypes of all types focus on, even if they avoid it or are ambivalent about it.

Self-preservation subtypes
Areas of focus: Physical needs, sustaining oneself, survival, safety, security, trust, danger, finances, resources, structure, control

Self-preservation subtypes tend to be more physically active and more anxious.

Social subtypes
Areas of focus: Belonging, community, groups, social relationships, group bonding, influence, social position, social duty

Social subtypes tend to be more intellectual and attuned to their social environments.

One-to-one subtypes
Areas of focus: Relationships between them and one other person, affection, intimacy, one-to-one bonding, attraction

One-to-one subtypes tend to be more intense, emotional and energetic.

Once the team members' subtypes are known, these can be placed on the Enneagram types on the Enneagram symbol using color-coded sticky dots. For example, brown for self-preservation subtypes, blue for social subtypes, and red for one-to-one subtypes. The analysis and discussion can be illuminating. Here's how to think about it in a similar way to mapping the Centers of Intelligence represented on a team.

Balance is the ideal, so are certain subtypes over- or under-presented within the team? With few self-preservation subtypes, does the team pay enough attention to structure, resources and control?

With few social subtypes, is the team sufficiently focused on the team as a whole? What about the extent to which the team creates a sense of belonging within the team or outside the team if they are team leaders of other teams? Do they pay attention to how team members influence one another, hopefully in constructive ways, or how they influence other parts of the organization?

With few one-to-one subtypes represented, do team members really know one another, and are they emotionally connected? This is just the start of the conversation.

What are the subtypes?

Subtypes are formed when the habitual emotional pattern of your type combines or intersects with one of the basic human instinctual drives that is most activated in you – self-preservation, social or, for one-to-one, intimacy. The type-based habitual emotional pattern then alters the activated instinct so our true needs in that instinctual area get thwarted or distorted. Here are some basic subtype descriptions.

Three subtypes for Ones
Habitual emotional pattern of anger

All Ones seek perfection and avoid mistakes. They experience anger as chronic dissatisfaction and irritation with the many things in life and work that are not as they should be, yet there are three distinct ways in which Ones manifest anger.

Self-preservation subtype Ones ("worry") focus on getting everything structured and organized correctly and experience anxiety, worry and anger in the form of irritation and frustration when they think this may not or is not occurring. Wanting to make sure that everything is under control, they emphasize precision and extreme accuracy as a way to make certain that everything is done right, feeling angry with themselves, others or situations when this does not occur.

Social subtype Ones ("non-adaptability") perceive themselves as role models who represent the right way of being and behaving. In their view, they set the standard as role models for how to be, and their anger arises when others do not respect them for this or do not live up to their example. Social subtype Ones also focus their efforts on correcting and perfecting social institutions, critiquing them, and manifesting anger when social systems and structures do not measure up to expectation.

One-to-one subtype Ones ("zeal") have a driving need to perfect others, particularly those who matter to them, as well as to perfect society in general. They perceive reforming others as both their right and their responsibility, and they go about this with intensity, passion and anger when people and society do not meet their expectations.

Three subtypes for Twos
Habitual emotional pattern of pride

All Twos have their sense of self-worth, personal pride and importance integrally linked with how others respond to them. They want to be viewed as appealing individuals who are valued for helping others and for being able to influence things in a positive direction. Pride can be thought of as an inflation or deflation of self-worth based on the reactions of others. As a result of this self-inflation, Twos can be thought of as perceiving themselves as Enneagram royalty, even Twos who may have suffered. As a result of self-deflation, Twos doubt their worth and value. There are three distinct ways in which Twos manifest pride.

Self-preservation subtype Twos ("me-first/privilege") deny their own needs for protection while, at the same time, try to attract others who will provide exactly that for them. Drawing others to them in the same way that children do – that is, by being appealing and appearing to be without guile – self-preservation Twos take pride in being able to do this and, at the same time, are also ambivalent about close relationships. They are also less trusting than social subtype or one-to-one subtype Twos.

Social subtype Twos ("ambition") focus on helping groups more than individuals and are more intellectually oriented and more comfortable being in visibly powerful positions than individuals of the other two subtype variations. Social subtype Twos are less concerned with how specific individuals respond to them and more focused on group-level reactions, which is a result of their desire to stand above the crowd in some way, feeling pride when this occurs. Social subtype Twos feel they must continuously prove that they have earned the right to an elevated social position through their action on behalf of groups and systems, while also appearing as if they have not made a great effort to do so.

One-to-one subtype Twos ("aggression/seduction") are primarily oriented to individual relationships and meeting the needs of important people and partners. They take pride in being able to attract specific individuals as a way of getting their own needs met – that is, they feel they have value or worth when chosen by someone important – but they are also highly motivated to meet the needs of these individuals as a way of developing and sustaining the relationship. One-to-one Twos have little need to prove it or justify their worth other than by providing attention and support to key individuals in their lives.

Three subtypes for Threes
Habitual emotional pattern of deceit

All Threes feel they must appear successful in order to gain the admiration and respect of others. They avoid failure in any form by hiding parts of themselves that do not conform to their image of success, deceiving not only others but also themselves. Threes come to believe that the image they create is actually who they are. Thus, deceit starts first with self-deceit. There are three distinct ways in which Threes manifest deceit.

Self-preservation subtype Threes ("security") want to be seen as self-reliant, autonomous, and hardworking, thus portraying an image of being a good or ideal person. The self-preservation Three creates an image of having no image and, therefore, may not even perceive this image as a form of deceit.

Social subtype Threes ("prestige") exhibit deceit because they want to be seen as successful and admirable in the context of specific social reference groups – that is, the groups in which they want to be admired, perceived as successful and be included. To this end, social subtype Threes continuously try to bolster their image by not acknowledging or revealing aspects of themselves such as feelings of anxiety, not knowing how to do something and more. They also like to be around other successful people because this proximity reinforces the social subtype Three's image and status.

One-to-one subtype Threes ("masculinity/femininity") want to be viewed as successful by specific individuals who are very important to them, primarily by appearing attractive to these people in some way, but also by helping these important people achieve their own success. Their deceit comes in the form of not acknowledging parts of themselves, or not showing aspects of themselves, that might not be attractive to these others.

Three subtypes for Fours
Habitual emotional pattern of envy

All Fours desire a feeling of deep connection both with their own interior worlds and with other people. When this doesn't happen, they feel deficient or not good enough. Because they believe something is lacking within them – although they cannot define exactly what this is – Fours consciously and unconsciously compare themselves to others (referred to as envy) as a way to determine what is wrong. As a result of these continuous comparisons, Fours feel superior to others, deficient in some way or both. They also suffer from doing this. There are three distinct ways in which Fours manifest envy.

Self-preservation subtype Fours ("reckless/dauntless") try to bear their suffering in silence as a way to prove that they are good enough by virtue of enduring their inner anguish. In addition, they engage in nonstop activity and/or reckless behavior as a way to feel excited and energized and to avoid not feeling as good as others. Of all three subtypes of type Four, self-preservation Fours do not appear to be as envious or deeply sensitive as the other two subtypes of Four because their constant comparisons – envy – are more subsurface.

Social subtype Fours ("shame") focus more on their deficiencies and also on earning the understanding and appreciation of the groups to which they belong. They want understanding and appreciation for their suffering and sorrows and desire acknowledgment for their heartfelt contributions to groups. At the same time, they often feel marginal to or not fully part of groups. Social subtype Fours are usually more aware of their envy.

One-to-one subtype Fours ("competition") feel compelled to express their needs and feelings outwardly and can be highly competitive with others to gain attention, to be heard, and to be acknowledged for their perspectives and accomplishments. Winning is perceived as another avenue for being understood, and coming out on top is seen as a way to resolve their continuous comparisons – envy – with others. In other words, someone who wins must be better than the others and not deficient.

Three subtypes for Fives
Habitual emotional pattern of avarice

All Fives have an intense need to acquire knowledge and wisdom and a similarly strong desire to avoid intrusion and loss of energy. They guard and preserve everything that they think they will need – for example, information, physical space, emotional privacy, personal energy and resources. There are three distinct ways in which Fives manifest the above, which is called avarice.

Self-preservation subtype Fives ("castle") are primarily concerned with being intruded upon and being overextended physically and energetically. They are trying to avoid the experience of feeling totally overwhelmed and drained to such an extent that they feel entirely depleted. For this reason, they hoard their involvement with others in the same way they are avaricious about their scarce resources.

Social subtype Fives ("totem") want to find and develop strong connections with groups that share their super-ideals, but they become disengaged when forced to live in a way that is not aligned with these higher-order beliefs. They focus on the group in search of extraordinary people, then are avaricious about these relationships, their shared ideals and, in the Five's view, their superior values.

One-to-one subtype Fives ("confidence") search for a strong, deep connection with another person whom they can trust and share confidences with, then are avaricious about what they share with people other than this special person, as well as avaricious with regard to sharing this other person or any special relationships with others.

Three subtypes for Sixes
Habitual emotional pattern of fear

All Sixes seek meaning, certainty and trust, hoping that the best is possible, yet simultaneously feeling fear that this will not happen. They doubt that others are trustworthy and/or whether they themselves are capable of meeting the challenges involved. There are three distinct ways in which Sixes manifest fear.

Self-preservation subtype Sixes ("warmth") manifest fear as an intense need to feel protected from danger, often seeking the family or a surrogate family to provide this. Self-preservation Sixes also use warmth and friendliness as a way to attract and maintain these types of relationships and support groups, all for the purpose of making themselves feel safe.

Social subtype Sixes ("duty") deal with fear by focusing on the rules, regulations and prescribed ways of behaving within their environment in an attempt to keep their own behavior in the acceptable range. They try to make sure they do nothing that will cause authority figures to chastise or punish them for going astray. They also feel responsible for the groups to which they belong and do their duty on the behalf of the group.

One-to-one subtype Sixes ("strength/beauty") are generally the most counter-phobic or counter-fear. They express their fear primarily through the denial of their anxieties and vulnerabilities by pushing against the fear, appearing bold, confident and sometimes fierce. They can also engage in physical or verbal behavior that makes them feel and appear highly courageous. This can be thought of as anti-fear generated by the avoidance of fear.

Three subtypes for Sevens
Habitual emotional pattern of gluttony

All Sevens have an insatiable thirst or gluttony for new stimulation of all kinds and distract themselves with interesting people, ideas and pleasurable experiences. This continuous stimulation and excitement allow them to avoid their fear of painful emotions, difficult situations and the imposition of limitations and restrictions. There are three distinct ways in which Sevens manifest gluttony.

Self-preservation subtype Sevens ("keepers of the castle") are gluttonous about creating close networks of family, friends and colleagues, not only to keep themselves feeling stimulated and secure but also to generate novel and exciting opportunities to pursue. To this end, they easily engage others to join them in their new ventures.

Social subtype Sevens ("sacrifice") sacrifice some of their gluttonous needs for stimulation in service of the group or of some ideal that is extremely important to them. At the same time, they are aware of wanting to pursue their desires but choose to postpone them momentarily and want to be explicitly thanked or acknowledged for this sacrifice. They do, however, go after and satisfy their desire later on.

One-to-one subtype Sevens ("suggestibility/fascination") are dreamers, with a need to see the stark reality of the world through rose-colored glasses. They are the most optimistic of the three subtypes of type Seven. Often, they become fascinated with one other person, become satiated with that person over time, then find someone new who intrigues and stimulates them. They may also forgo romantic relationships entirely because their gluttony is in the form of romantic, idealized dreaming. The dream is often better than the reality.

Three subtypes for Eights
Habitual emotional pattern of lust

Eights pursue justice and control, but also deny their anxiety, sadness or any sense of weakness. The way Eights avoid these feelings and vulnerabilities is to engage in a variety of self-satisfying behaviors and do so in an excessive way. This excessiveness is what is meant by lust. For example, they take big and immediate action, work superhuman hours, eat too much food or too little, exercise for three hours a day for a week and then don't exercise for two months and more. There are three distinct ways in which Eights manifest lust.

Self-preservation subtype Eights ("survival") focus their excessiveness or lust on getting what they need for survival, and they become highly frustrated, intolerant, and angry when the fulfillment of these needs is thwarted. Of the three Eight subtypes, the self-preservation subtype Eights tend to speak the least and to approach situations – particularly those they deem important to their survival – in a highly strategic way that allows them to get the upper hand. They are especially attuned to influence networks.

Social subtype Eights ("solidarity") vigorously protect others from unjust and unfair authorities and systems and challenge social norms. At the same time, they seek power, influence and sometimes pleasure. Wanting loyalty from others and being highly loyal themselves, they derive a feeling of power from challenging others as well as from defending those under their protection, which makes them feel less vulnerable. Their lust is in the form of excessiveness for groups and causes where they become central to them, often organizing or leading them.

One-to-one subtype Eights ("possession") are the most intense, rebellious and emotional of the three Eight subtypes. Provocative and passionate in a way that draws others toward them, these Eights derive their power and influence from being at the center of things, from the strong and energetic connections they develop, and from the fervent way in which they express their positions and values. They are lustful and possessive of those with whom they are intimate or close.

Three subtypes for Nines
Habitual emotional pattern of laziness

In order to maintain harmony and comfort and to avoid conflict, Nines numb themselves to their own reactions by not paying attention to their own deeper feelings, needs and impulses. This self-numbing, called laziness, disables them from knowing what they think, feel and want, and what action is the right one to take. There are three distinct ways in which Nines manifest laziness.

Self-preservation subtype Nines ("appetite") use the comfort of repetitive routines and pleasant activities as a way of not paying attention to themselves; thus, they use routine and comforting and rhythmic activities and experiences as their form of laziness about self. These repetitive activities also distract self-preservation Nines from dealing with more important issues, such as their own feelings and needs. In addition, many self-preservation Nines also acquire (have an appetite for) collections, and their desire for these objects increases the more they obtain. They find these collections comforting and pleasing.

Social subtype Nines ("participation") work extremely hard on behalf of a group, organization or cause that they support or belong to as a way of not focusing on themselves; thus, they use working hard and merging with a group as their form of laziness about self. Social subtype Nines are usually very friendly, and their need to feel a part of things is rooted in their underlying feeling of not fitting in. Thus, social subtype Nines sacrifice themselves in the service of others, rarely showing the pain, stress and overwork they experience as a result.

One-to-one subtype Nines ("fusion/union") join or merge with others who are important to them as a way of not paying attention to their own thoughts, feelings and needs. This fusion with others results in one-to-one subtype Nines becoming disconnected from their own deep desires and confusing their own sense of self and fulfillment with the desires and gratification of those with whom they have merged. In this way, they use fusion with specific others as their form of laziness about self.

ENNEAGRAM TESTS

Enneagram tests can be the beginning of the conversation to explore type. However, if you want to use a test, please remember that none of them are 100% accurate.

Four most frequently used Enneagram tests for purchase

iEQ9 (Dirk Cloete)

A series of questions to answer, with different reports to choose from. As you answer the questions, the more precise the questions become.

WEPSS (Jerry Wagner PhD)

A series of questions to answer, with sufficient standardization, reliability and validity to be included and favorably reviewed in Buros's Mental Measurements Yearbook – a respected authority in the test field. After taking the test you receive a report with scores on the positive and negative features of your core type, plus more.

RHETI (The Enneagram Institute)

A series of forced-choice questions with paired statements, plus a profile report; the most used Enneagram test that has been available for several decades; the long version of the RHETI is more accurate than the short version.

Frequently used free Enneagram test

Eclecticenergies.com (Ewald Berkers et al)

A free online test that sends an email of the test-taker's score, plus a description of that type; the original version is more accurate than the newer version.

RECOMMENDED BOOKS, WEBSITES AND MORE

Enneagram books

Enneagram introduction

The Art of Typing by Ginger Lapid-Bogda PhD

Describes, through words and illustration, the nine type-based ego structures and how to differentiate between them

The Art of the Enneagram by Ginger Lapid-Bogda PhD and Russell (Tres) Bogda

Through graphics and words, takes you on the journey of each type

Enneagram by Helen Palmer

A classic and foundational Enneagram book

Comprehensive Enneagram overview

The Complete Enneagram by Beatrice Chestnut PhD

A comprehensive description of the 27 Enneagram subtypes, plus more

The Wisdom of the Enneagram by Don Riso and Russ Hudson

A thorough explanation of each type, including type-based levels of development

Nine Lenses on the World by Jerry Wagner PhD

Covers the full array of Enneagram theory

Enneagram in organizations

Bringing Out the Best in Yourself at Work by Ginger Lapid-Bogda PhD

Describes the nine types in action in a variety of contexts: communication, feedback, conflict, leadership, and teams

What Type of Leader Are You? by Ginger Lapid-Bogda PhD

Describes the nine types in action in eight specific leadership competencies

Bringing Out the Best in Everyone You Coach by Ginger Lapid-Bogda PhD

Describes the best way to coach people of each Enneagram type

Consulting with the Enneagram by Ginger Lapid-Bogda PhD

Integrates the Enneagram with the consulting process from beginning to end

The Enneagram Development Guide by Ginger Lapid-Bogda PhD

50+ development activities for each type based on development areas

The Leadership Dance by Richard Knowles

A different way of using the Enneagram to design teams and organizations

The Process Enneagram: Essays on Theory and Practice edited by Richard Knowles

Practical accounts of how to use the Process Enneagram

Spiritual Enneagram

Spiritual Dimensions of the Enneagram by Sandra Maitri

A robust explanation of the spiritual aspects of each type, with a focus on the Holy Ideas, the higher mental state for each type

Keys to the Enneagram by A.H Almaas

A tour of the nine types with type-based guidance for increasing consciousness

Books about teams

The Wisdom of Teams by Jon Katzenbach and Douglas Smith

A classic approach to teams and teamwork

Paradoxes of Group Life by Kenwyn Smith and David Berg

A fascinating analysis about the undercurrents and unconscious of groups and teams

Safe Enough to Soar: Accelerating Trust, Inclusion & Collaboration in the Workplace by Fred Miller and Judith Katz

Explains how to foster teaming, especially, but not only, in the context of Diversity

Consulting books

Flawless Consulting by Peter Block

The classic book on consulting, especially related to contracting for work with clients

The Trusted Advisor by David Maister

How to move from consultant as "vendor" to consultant as "strategic partner"

Enneagram websites

Enneagram information

Selected websites offering a breadth and depth of accurate Enneagram information

TheEnneagramInBusiness.com

The site of Ginger Lapid-Bogda PhD, providing information about the Enneagram system and types as well as business applications and organizational resources

EnneagramWorldwide.com

The site of the Enneagram in the Narrative Tradition providing information about the Enneagram system and types

TheEnneagramatWork.com

The site of Peter O'Hanrahan, providing information about the Enneagram system, types and personal and professional applications

EnneagramSpectrum.com

The site of Jerry Wagner PhD, providing information about the Enneagram system, theory, types and applications

Conscious.tv

A site with a robust Enneagram section, providing Enneagram type panels with three to five people of the same type interviewed by Iain McNay or Renate McNay

EnneagramLearningPortal.com

Subscription-based eLearning from The Enneagram in Business

Enneagram apps

Know Your Type | enneagramapp.com

Available on IOS (Apple) and Kindle (Amazon). This app contains an animated typing section as well as an array of other interactive Enneagram information and applications

Enneagram professional certificate programs and training tools

TheEnneagramInBusiness.com

Provides multiple professional certificate programs, including two coaching programs that are ICF (International Coaching Federation) accredited and three Train-the-Trainer programs that teach how to bring the Enneagram into organizations. There are additional programs to refine your typing skills or deepen your development. All programs are IEA (International Enneagram Association) accredited.

TheEnneagramInBusiness.com

Training tools

28 full-color, hard copy training tools for a wide variety of Enneagram-business applications

8 full-color, virtual training tools for different Enneagram-business applications

EnneagramLearningPortal.com
Enneagram Learning Portal (ELP)

An interactive subscription-based platform to learn the Enneagram, professional uses for coaches, trainers and consultants, and a variety of organizational applications

ABOUT THE AUTHOR, GINGER LAPID-BOGDA PHD

Ginger Lapid-Bogda, an internationally recognized Enneagram author, trainer, keynote speaker, organization development consultant and coach, is considered a world leader in bringing the insights of the Enneagram to organizations across the globe. She designs and delivers custom programs for organizations in a wide variety of industries. Author of nine Enneagram books, she also offers global certification programs and 28 full-color training tools. In addition, Ginger is a long-time member of NTL (National Training Labs), past president of the IEA (International Enneagram Association), and her two En-neagram-based coaching certificate programs are both ICF (International Coaching Federation) and IEA accredited. You can find more information on her website, TheEnneagraminBusiness.com. info@theenneagraminbusiness.com

Ginger's clients (partial list)

Genentech-Roche, Salesforce, Apple, Facebook, Greenville Health System, Center for Creative Leadership, LeasePlan, Kaiser Permanente, Hudson Institute of Coaching, US Airforce, Hewlett Packard, Nestlé, Toyota, Sun Microsystems, Cisco, Kaiser Permanente, and numerous small businesses, consulting firms, government agencies and law firms

About the illustrator, Gwen Baker-Yuill

Gwen Baker-Yuill, based in Bend, Oregon, has worn many professional "hats" throughout her career. Her varied background includes commercial sculpting for companies such as Disney, Mattel and Warner Brothers, and she has drawn, painted and illustrated for over 35 years. In addition, Gwen has also taught English, art and theater in both high school and middle school. Recently, she has specialized in program management and online education, focusing on website design, curriculum development, marketing, customer support, grant writing, and faculty coordination. She currently works as the operations manager at The Enneagram in Business. gwen@theenneagraminbusiness.com

About the Enneagram in Business

Founded in 2004 by Ginger Lapid-Bogda PhD, The Enneagram in Business is dedicated to increasing competence and consciousness in organizations worldwide using the Enneagram, often integrated with other time-tested and innovative approaches. We serve to increase both capability and possibility at the individual, leadership, team, organizational and community levels. To this end, we offer best-in-class resources needed to bring the Enneagram to organizations. These include professional services for companies; professional certificate programs for trainers, coaches and consultants; 28 full-color hard copy training and 8 virtual training tools; the app "Know Your Type" for iOS; free Enneagram eBooks; and an online subscription-based Enneagram Learning Portal.

With a network of over 70 Enneagram professionals worldwide, we work in organizations of all sizes from all industries, including for-profit, non-profit, professional service organizations and government agencies. We adhere to Blue Ocean ethical standards of practice and values, including honesty, respect for intellectual property, open-source sharing, collaboration, fair pricing and client focus.

Enneagram books by Ginger Lapid-Bogda, PhD

Bringing Out the Best in Yourself at Work (2004) | core work applications of the Enneagram

What Type of Leader Are You? (2007) | develop leadership competencies using the Enneagram

Bringing Out the Best in Everyone You Coach (2010) | high-impact coaching using the Enneagram

The Enneagram Development Guide (2011) | 50+ powerful development activities for each Enneagram type

Consulting with the Enneagram (2015) | a systematic structure for achieving powerful results with clients

The Enneagram Coloring Book (2016) | a right and left-brained way to learn the Enneagram